Sophie Arnould

Adolphe Lalauze, Robert B Douglas

BIBLIOLIFE

SOPHIE ARNOULD

ACTRESS AND WIT

BY

ROBERT B. DOUGLAS

WITH

SEVEN COPPER-PLATE ENGRAVINGS

BY

ADOLPHE LALAUZE

PARIS
CHARLES CARRINGTON
13, FAUBOURG MONTMARTRE
MDCCCXCVIII

PREFACE

To apologise for submitting a Life of the gifted creature, Sophie Arnould, to the suffrages of the English public would be an act of pure affectation. A popular favourite caressed and beloved in her own day, she still possesses a charm for the "children of men".

All feel that Macaulay was right in not dwelling too exclusively "on battles and sieges, the rise and fall of administrations, intrigues in the palace, or on debates in the parliament", for the simple reason that these things fail to represent the people and times as they really were or are. Public amusements, he thought, were one of the best exponents of the taste and progress of a nation. I venture to share his view. Nowhere are the feelings of the public more vividly depicted than at the theatre, or the opera. Sophie Arnould, looked at in this light, strikes us as the most brilliant woman of her time, who portrayed its ideas and manners more effectively perhaps, than could many tomes of philosophical theory.

To me she appears a typical representative of the Frenchwoman of the latter half of the 18th century. She possessed all the qualities, good and bad, which marked the women of her generation, and it should not be forgotten that that generation of women comprised the sisters

and wives of the men who made the Revolution—the
mothers of the men who aided Napoleon to found the
Empire. I may mention incidentally that one of Sophie
Arnould's sons became Colonel of a regiment of Cuirassiers,
and was killed while leading a charge at the battle of
Wagram

As an individual, too, her career presents some attractions for the biographer. Carlyle complained that the
only lives worth reading were those of players, and
Sophie Arnould was the greatest lyric and dramatic artist
of her day She was brought into contact with all the
literary giants of the time, and was for years one of the
leaders of Parisian society. As for her witticisms, they
are still quoted almost every day in French journals and
magazines To be *the* acknowledged wit in perhaps the
wittiest age of a country, believing itself to possess a
monopoly of refined humour, is to achieve a certain
distinction

These considerations, coupled with the fact that the
name of Sophie Arnould, though familiar enough to her
countrymen, is comparatively unknown to English readers,
caused me to undertake the task of writing her life. It
was a difficult work, and has occupied all my spare time,
in the intervals of other literary work, for two years.
Much research was required, for the only modern book
about Sophie Arnould, brilliantly written as it undoubtedly
is (by MM. E and J de Goncourt) is not only devoid
of all chronological arrangement, but often contains serious
blunders.

Just as my object, in writing the "Life and Times
of Madame du Barry", was to prove that the much
maligned "Jeanne" after all was far from being so
"black" as she had been "painted", so in this effort
to record the life of the volatile butterfly, Sophie

Arnould, has my aim been to show that beneath
the apparent fickleness of the actress beat the heart of
a loving woman, and that, if the mordant satire of her
tongue sometimes stung like a wasp, it was but a trick
to dissipate the echo of the word of gracious kindness
she had just elsewhere spoken. If to her imputed
faults I have been "a little blind", and to the virtues
others deny her, "rather over kind", let it be put down
to the sympathy I feel for this much misunderstood
woman. During twice twelve months her words have
been to me a source of inspiration and pleasure. Again
one heard, while bending over dust-covered manuscripts,
the quick-winged shafts of clever satire, saw the sparkle
in the mischievous eyes, or caught the momentary betrayal
of a shade of sadness lurking in the corner of the mobile
mouth, or anon was enchanted with the peal of mocking
laughter, clear as crystal, that broke from her lips. I
shall be rewarded if the perusal of this little "booke"
gives to others half as much satisfaction as the writing
of it has afforded me. This attempt to present Sophie
Arnould as the superlatively charming, baffling, indescribable character she actually was, falls, I feel full well,
far short of the reality. The only credit I claim is for
having introduced to the English reader, for the first
time, a personage hitherto known to them merely by
name, and whose career appeared to me--as I hope it
will appear to them—to present features of no inconsiderable interest.

Finally, it would be sheer ingratitude on my part to
omit thanking M. Adolphe Lalauze for his illustrations,
full of charm and *finesse*, which will surely form another
wreath to his fame as a master of his subtle craft.
Anatole France once said that Lalauze " constantly
revealed an abundance of ingenious ideas, as well as

a remarkable facility for supple and brilliant work."
What men, who are vastly more capable than I am
of estimating the *technique* of his varied talent at its
real worth, think of him, may be seen in Beraldi's work
on "Les Graveurs du XIX Siècle". I also beg to thank
Mr. Charles Carrington, who originated the happy idea
of inviting the co-operation of Lalauze, for the honour
he has conferred upon my small effort by going to
great expense and pains to produce it in so grand a
style. He is already regarded as one of the rising *libraire-*
éditeurs of Paris, and will undoubtedly prove no mean
rival to the "Conquets" and "Ferrouds", who have
given so many beautiful works to the world of book-
amateurs and bibliophiles.

ROBERT B. DOUGLAS.

January 1st, 1898.

CONTENTS

CHAPTER I.

SOPHIE ARNOULD

CHAPTER I.

Bibliography—Birth—Education—Introduced to the Queen and Madame de Pompadour—A true prophecy—Ordered to join the Opera Company—Her mother tries to make her enter a Convent—Proposed marriage—Début at the Opera—Her stage-professors—Favourable reception—A lucky omen—La Provençale—First appearance in tragic opera—Enée et Lavinie—A modest author—Favourable criticisms—Les Fêtes de Paphos—A joint production—Charles Collé—An incorrect diagnosis.

(1740—1758)

GRIMM writes under the date of February, 1758, "The Opéra Comique has made an acquisition this winter, and crowds have been attracted to the performances to see Mlle Arnould, a young actress

aged sixteen, and very pretty. The beauty of her
voice, added to her desire to please and anxiety
to improve, cause those who like this kind of entertainment to indulge in the highest expectations
concerning her." *

These expectations were fully realized. For more
than twenty years Sophie Arnould was one of the
brightest ornaments of the French operatic stage.
Her voice, there is reason to believe, was rather
thin in quality, and was certainly worn out before
she was forty, but it was capable of expressing
pathos and feeling in a manner which was then
entirely new to an audience.

A beautiful voice and considerable dramatic talent
would not, however, have sufficed to prevent the
name of Sophie Arnould from falling, in the course
of a century, into something like oblivion; but she
had a rare but dangerous gift, which, if it made her
many enemies in her lifetime, has in return given
her a certain degree of celebrity. She was very
witty, and her wit was of that caustic, biting nature
which makes its owners more dreaded than beloved.
Even now—more than a hundred years after she
retired into private life—her brilliant sarcasms are
continually being quoted in papers and magazines.

Her sayings were collected, and published in 1813,
eleven years after her death, in a book called *Arnoldiana*, to which was prefixed a biographical sketch,

which, though slight and very far from complete, relates the most salient events of her life. The book, apparently, was successful, for in the course of the same year there was published "Esprit de Sophie Arnould," a very thin 18mo. of less than 100 pages. It is believed by Quérard to be by "Favrolle"— one of the pseudonyms of the Baronne de Mère (Mlle Guénard) an indefatigable literary hack who, in less than thirty years, produced more than a hundred works (in 320 volumes), a few of which were intended for "the instruction of youth," and the great majority for "the amusement of the barracks." The "Esprit of Sophie Arnould" could not certainly have given its author much trouble. A few words of introduction, a score of the best known anecdotes of Sophie Arnould, and a couple of her letters, suffice to fill up its few small pages, which contain little or nothing that is not better told in "Arnoldiana." *

No further addition was made to the bibliography of Sophie Arnould till 1837, when Comte de La-mothe-Langon published the *Memoirs of Sophie Arnould*. The historical value of this production may be estimated from the fact that in the Catalogue of the Bibliothèque Nationale the entry relating to this book concludes with the words "see Novels." About twenty years later, the Brothers de Goncourt

---

* *Arnoldiana* is generally believed to be the work of a writer named Deville

discovered, amongst a parcel of odds and ends
they had bought from a dealer in autographs, eight
or ten letters written by Sophie Arnould. They at
once set to work and produced a monograph on
the witty actress, incorporating therein the letters
they had so fortunately acquired. Their *Sophie
Arnould* appeared in 1857, and has been republished
several times since, the latest edition bearing the
date 1885. Perhaps it may be little short of a
literary heresy to hint that those two accomplished
writers have ever touched anything they did not adorn,
but it may reasonably be doubted whether they are
quite as much at home in collecting data, and re-
conciling contradictory accounts, as they are in works
affording a greater scope to the imagination.

These few books constitute all that have been
written concerning Sophie Arnould, but occasional
mention of her name is to be found in the letters
or Memoirs of Voltaire, Grimm, Marmontel, Collé,
and many other writers, and some information regarding her and her fellow-actresses is to be derived
from modern works on the French Stage in the
Eighteenth Century.

The few autobiographical notes left by Sophie
Arnould are certainly incorrect as to the date and
place of her birth. " In a letter, first published in
1776, she declares that she was born in the alcove
in which Admiral Coligny was assassinated two hundred years before." The hotel which Coligny in-

habited was in the Rue Béthizy,—a small street that was destroyed when the Rue de Rivoli was constructed —and though the parents of Mlle Arnould did occupy the rooms in which the great Huguenot had lived, it was not until some years after the birth of their eldest daughter, Sophie.

The other statement contained in the same letter, —that she was born on February 14, 1745,—is also incorrect as to the year, and perhaps also as to the day. Messrs. de Goncourt discovered in the National Archives the following extract from the register of the Church of St. Roch:

"The year One thousand seven-hundred-and-forty, the 14th of February, Magdeleine Sophie, daughter of Jean Arnould, here present, and of Rose Marguerite Laurent his wife, born yesterday Rue Louis le Grand in this parish, has been baptised. Godparents: Louis Le Vasseur, manager of the King's farms, Rue Coq Héron in the parish of Saint Eustache, and Magdeleine Chevalier, spinster, rue du Mail in the above named parish."

Jean Arnould and his wife had five children; two sons and three daughters. Magdeleine Sophie was the eldest daughter. Her younger sister, Rosalie, also displayed great talent in music, and was one of the Chamber Musicians of the King from 1770 to 1792.

The father of Sophie Arnould appears to have been a quiet, respectable *bourgeois*, sufficiently intelligent to carry on his business, which according to the author of "Arnoldiana" was that of an inn-keeper, * but not a clever or intellectual man. His wife, on the contrary, evinced a great liking for literary society. She numbered amongst her friends, or at least acquaintances, Voltaire, Fontenelle, Diderot, and d'Alembert, and perhaps she discussed philosophy with them.

Their conversation so impressed her with the advantages of education that she resolved to make her children prodigies of learning. As soon as ever Sophie could talk, her education began, and as the child was precocious, and learned readily, she could soon read and write, play the spinet, and sing. She commenced to learn music when she was only two and a half, and when she was seven or eight could read music at sight without any difficulty. When she was little more than four she had already, and without any trouble, learned to read, and by the time she was seven, wrote a better hand than she did when she was grown up,—though perhaps that was not difficult

Mme Arnould was proud of such an accomplished child, and engaged the best professors to teach Sophie all the necessary arts and accomplishments. Being exceedingly apt and quick, the child soon learned whatever her professors could teach her, and, amongst other things, was able to speak and write her own language correctly which, in that age, few persons except literary men and women could do.

According to other accounts he did not become an inn-keeper till some years later

When the Opera house was burned down, one of the ladies of the Court asked Mlle Arnould if she could give her any particulars concerning " *cette* terrible incendie."

" All that I am able to tell you, Madam," replied the actress, " is that *incendie* is a masculine noun."

At ten, Sophie Arnould, according to her own account at least, " sang like a professional ", and when she was twelve was familiar with Latin and Italian. Her talents were not long destined to lie hidden. On one occasion the child sang a portion of the mass at Vesper service at the Val de Grace. The Princess of Modena, who chanced to be present, was so struck with the beauty of the voice, and sympathy and pathos put into the words, that she persuaded many of her aristocratic friends to visit the church, and at last the Queen (Marie Leczinska) heard of this wonderful singer, and desired that the girl might be brought to Versailles to sing before her

The Princess of Modena had no difficulty in persuading Madame Arnould to let her daughter go, and Sophie was taken to Versailles. Though only a child, she had all the confidence and self-possession of the finished *artiste*, and was not at all intimidated by the presence of her royal auditor. The Queen was delighted, and expressed a wish that the girl should be one of her Musicians of the Chamber.

But though Marie Leczinska was nominally Queen

of France, the power which should have pertained
to that position was practically possessed by Madame
de Pompadour, the King's mistress, who had also
expressed a wish to hear Sophie Arnould sing, and
of course her wishes had to be obeyed, but the
Princess of Modena did not consider that it was
quite etiquette for her to present her *protégée* to
both the crowned and uncrowned queens of France,
so Madame Arnould had to introduce her daughter
to the favourite.

An account of this interview was written by Sophie
Arnould some years afterwards, and certainly bears
the impress of truthfulness, for it begins by mentioning that Madame de Pompadour, after conversing
with her visitors for a few moments, left the room,
first telling them that they were not to speak or
move until her return. This was a very usual trick
with the favourite, who liked to impress people with
the belief that the King might come in at any
moment, and that he would be exceedingly annoyed
if he found any company present when he wished to
consult his mistress on State affairs.

Little Sophie Arnould, however, cared next to
nothing for either the King or his mistress, and
walking up to one of the spinets—there were two
or three in the room—ran her fingers over the keys
and began to sing.

Madame de Pompadour re-entered the room, and
listened, entranced, to the girl's singing. At the

end of the song she came forward, patted Sophie gently on the cheek, and said:

"My dear child, you will make a charming princess."

Madame Arnould, in spite of her taste for *philosophedom* and her fondness for the society of men of letters, was at heart a *bourgeoise*, and did not appreciate this equivocal compliment.

"I do not understand you, Madam," she said, in her stiffest manner. "My daughter is not of sufficiently good station to ever become a *real* princess, and she is far too well brought up ever to become a *stage* princess."

The King's mistress, it may well be imagined, smiled at this tirade. She had already mentally resolved that Sophie should be engaged at the Opera, and her wishes were law. Only a very few days after the visit to Versailles Mme Arnould received a letter bearing the royal seal. This letter was to inform her that she and her daughter were appointed private musicians to the Queen. A few hours later came another official document, announcing that Mlle Sophie Arnould was named one of the musicians to His Majesty the King, and would be required to sing at the Opera.

This last communication was not at all to the liking of Sophie's mother. She did not mind her daughter singing before the good and virtuous Marie Leczinska, but no girl could hope to preserve her

chastity at the Opera. Rather than see her child
ruined, she determined to put Sophie in a convent,
and went off at once to the Abbess of Panthémont.
But the Abbess, when she heard the facts of the
case, firmly refused to admit the girl within the
walls of the convent. It was dangerous enough to
run counter to the King's wishes, but it was a
hundred times worse to oppose Madame de Pompadour. At two other convents the same reply was
given, and Madame Arnould began to perceive that
she would have to make the best of a bad bargain.

There is a story in the unpublished memoirs of
Sophie Arnould to the effect that her mother wished
to marry her to an old man, the Chevalier de
Malezieux, who was so enamoured of her that he
would have settled upon her 40,000 livres a year.
But if Madame Arnould was bent on this match,
Sophie was just as much opposed to it, and her
father did not view it very favourably, or at any
rate did not exert his parental authority to force
his daughter into a marriage which was distasteful
to her.

As Sophie could neither be received into a convent or married, there was no alternative but to
comply with the King's commands, and allow the
girl to enter the Opera Company. Madame de
Conti endeavoured to persuade Madame Arnould
that her daughter would not be called upon, at least
for some months, to appear at the Opera, but would

only have to sing at the Concerts of Sacred Music.

The managers of the Opera, however, were not doing very good business, and being anxious to try any thing that was likely to hit the public taste, Mlle Arnould was sent on to sing an incidental song in a ballet.

It was the 15th of December, 1757, when Sophie made her first bow to the public. Actors and actresses, even in the present day, attach a superstitious meaning to the first words they are called upon to pronounce upon the stage, or to the first words uttered in a new theatre. The piece in which Sophie Arnould made her appearance was a ballet by Mouret entitled, *Les Amours des Dieux*, and the first words of her song were *Charmant amour*,—a not inappropriate omen for one who was to become notorious for her gallantries.

Even with this restricted opportunity to show her talents, she at once became a popular favourite. Her voice, according to all accounts, was not powerful, but sweet, and she possessed the comparatively rare gift of being able to throw into it wonderful expression and pathos. She had been taught acting by Mlle Clairon, the greatest tragic actress of the day, and had received finishing lessons in singing from Mlle Fel, and was an apt and intelligent pupil, possessed of true dramatic instinct, and, though young and inexperienced, absolutely free from the terrors of nervousness and stage fright. These qualities, com-

bined with her beauty, quickly gave her the position
of a "star." Thursday became the fashionable night
at the Opera because it was one of the nights on
which she appeared, and whenever she sang the
Opera house was so crowded that Fréron said that
people "took as much trouble to get into the Opera,
as they would to get into Paradise."

The second piece in which Sophie Arnould appeared was entitled *La Provençale*; it was really an
additional act inserted in an opera-ballet by Lafont,
music by Mouret, called les Fêtes de Thalie, which
had been originally produced in 1714 and revived
in 1722 with the Provençale added. It was not
unusual in those days for an opera-ballet to consist
of three or four acts with an entirely fresh and
irrelevant story related in each act,—indeed not in-
frequently each act was by a different author, though
the whole of the music was by one composer. The
plot of this little operetta though very simple, doubtless offered opportunities of which a clever actress
would not be slow to avail herself. " A very beautiful
young woman is brought up from childhood in a
country house by the sea side. She knows so little
about her fellow-beings that her governess and an
old tutor have no difficulty in persuading her that
she is extremely ugly. She is undeceived by a young
man who falls in love with her, and who takes her
from the prison in which she is confined." *

Annale dramatiques, 1809 Vol. 4, p. 106.

On 13th April 1758 the young actress had her first opportunity of singing a long part—that of *Lavinia* in *Enée et Lavinie*, a tragic opera in five acts by Fontenelle, music by d'Auvergne The opera was an old one: it was first produced in 1690 with music by Colasse, a pupil of Lully. The composer was long since dead, but Fontenelle, who lived to almost complete his hundredth year, was still alive when d'Auvergne began to write fresh music for the opera. He told the old author of his intention, and Fontenelle replied, "Sir, you do me too much honour. It is now sixty years since that opera was first performed;—it was a failure, but I never heard that that was the fault of the composer."

D'Auvergne was not to be deterred from his purpose however, and had no reason to be dissatisfied with the result, though the success was probably due to Sophie Arnould. There were few dramatic critics in those days, but the newspapers of the time teem with her praise, and she is told that tragedy suits her even better than comedy, and that if she wants to excel in both she has but to listen to the voice of her own genius. Natural and touching grace, intelligence, animation. and expression that never borders on grimace, are other attributes bestowed; from which it will seen that Sophie Arnould was as great a favourite with the critics as she was with the public. She appears to have sometimes taken the part of *Lavinia* in this opera, and sometimes that of *Venus*;—perhaps she played them alternately.

Very soon after this time Sophie Arnould created a trio of small parts in an opera-ballet entitled *Les Fêtes de Paphos*. The music of this opera-ballet was by Mondonville, but the three acts were written by as many different pens. The first act *(Venus and Adonis)* was by Collet, "the secretary of some lord or other" and was "intensely stupid " The second act *(Bacchus and Erigone)* was by the late la Bruère, and was said to be "well written, but cold, not natural, and badly put together,"—which latter qualities must somewhat have detracted from the good writing. The third act—the title of which is not given,—was by far the most successful and the best written, and was by the Abbé Voisenon. Though not very particular—even for an Eighteenth Century Abbé,—Voisenon did not care about letting it be generally known that he was the author of the work, and consequently two or three other people claimed whatever credit there was attaching to the production. One of these claimants was Mondonville, who not content with having written the music for the opera, declared that he was also the author of this act. The Duc de la Vallière when he heard of this claim said:

"If Mondonville continues to say that he wrote that act, I swear I will go about telling everybody that I composed the music."

CH CARRINGTON EDITEUR

This anecdote, and the remarks on the play and its authors, are from the *Journal and Memoirs* of Charles Collé—who is not to be confounded with the Collet who wrote the first act, as mentioned above. He was a dramatist and literary man and literary secretary and reader to the Duc d'Orléans. One of his pieces, *La Chasse de Henri IV*, kept the stage for many years, and possibly would be acted occasionally even now but for political reasons. Collé was also very clever in composing nonsense verses. At the house of Madame de Jencin he once recited what purported to be a love-song but which really had no meaning whatever. Old Fontenelle— then considerably over ninety years of age—begged the author to repeat the verses, as he had failed to catch the sense on the first reading

"You great stupid," cried Madame de Jencin, "don't you know that it is all rubbish, and there is no sense in it to catch?"

"Indeed, Madam!" retorted the old poet. "I thought it sounded quite as sensible as anything else I ever hear at this house."

Collé witnessed the performance of this opera-ballet and does not appear to have been at all pleased with it, though he has nothing but praise for the actress.

"The music of this ballet was pitiable," he writes, "and it would not have run six nights if it had not been for a young actress who made her first appearance this winter, and who in four months has become the queen of this theatre. I have never seen combined in one actress so much grace, truthfulness to nature, sentiment, dignity, warmth, and intelligence. She can depict the deepest grief without her face losing one trace of its beauty. She would be twice as great an actress as Mlle Le Maure, if she only had two thirds of her voice, and Le Maure will always be regarded as a celebrated *artiste*. I speak of Mlle Sophie Arnould, who is not yet nineteen years of age, but they cannot hope to keep her long at the Opera, she has not the necessary strength. The managers are killing her, and I fear will not take long to do it." *

. Collé was a better critic than he was physican, or at all events was mistaken in his diagnosis in this instance, for Sophie Arnould continued to act for twenty years, and lived a quarter of a century after her retirement.

Collé, *Journal et Mémoires*, vol ii, p 147.

CHAPTER II.

PERHAPS one of the reasons which had partly reconciled Mme. Arnould to her daughter's career was that the salary would be extremely useful. Matters had not gone prosperously with the Arnoulds for some time past. M. Arnould had lost a great part of his money in some unfortunate speculation, and a long and serious illness had made a further heavy drain upon his diminished resources He had been obliged to remove from the Rue du Louvre to the Hotel de Lisieux in the Rue Béthisy, close to the Rue Fossé St. Germain l'Auxerrois, and had converted his new residence into an inn. A board over the door announced that country gentle- men visiting Paris could be accommodated with good bed-rooms at 30 *sous* a night.

Whether many country gentlemen availed themselves of this offer we cannot say, but very shortly
after Sophie made her *début* at the Opera, a new
lodger came to her father's hotel, and seemed
inclined to make a long stay. He was a young
man of about twenty-five, of aristocratic bearing,
but apt to be eccentric in his manners. He said
that his name was Dorval, that he was an artist
and a poet, and that he had come to Paris to study
art and get a play produced, and therefore what
more natural than that he should take apartments
in a house where such excellent literary society was
to be met?

It might have struck the Arnoulds that poets and
painters generally did much more work, and had
much less money than their new lodger, but as he
paid liberally and regularly, they probably never
troubled to enquire into the truth of his statements.
His clothes too were better than those worn by poor
poets, who do not generally indulge in a taste for
real lace. He also lived well, and constantly received
hampers of game, or choice wines, all of which he
begged the Arnould family to share with him.

In a very short time he had become quite a
friend of the family. He took his meals with them;
and in the evening he played backgammon with
M. Arnould, or discussed philosophy, or read the
latest poem to Mme. Arnould. Of Sophie he appeared
to take no notice, beyond the ordinary civilities of

good breeding, but he paid marked attention to her mother, who no doubt thought him a very sensible and well-bred young man, and was far from suspecting his intentions. This went on for some time. One night after Dorval had played his usual game of backgammon with M. Arnould, and had drawn tears from the eyes of Mme. Arnould by the way he had recited some touching verses, all retired to their rooms, but neither Dorval nor Sophie went to bed. As soon as all was still a carriage drove quietly up to the corner of the street, a valet descended and let himself into the Hotel de Lisieux by means of a duplicate key, crept noiselessly upstairs and scratched at Dorval's door. In a minute Dorval came out fully dressed; Sophie appeared from her room, the trio gently tip-toed downstairs, passed through the door, and in another minute were driving away.

Great must have been the consternation of Madame Arnould the next morning, when it was discovered that Sophie and Dorval were both missing, and had evidently eloped together. But in the course of the morning a lackey in a magnificent livery appeared, bearing a letter for Madame Arnould. The letter was signed by the Comte de Lauraguais. The writer said that he had long admired Sophie, and in order to win her had concealed his rank, and pretended to be a poet. He could not unfortunately marry Sophie, as he was married already, but if ever he should be left a widower, his first step would be to render legitimate his union with the only woman who had ever won his heart, etc., etc.

Poor Madame Arnould, who had boasted to Madame de Pompadour that her daughter was far too well brought up to become a stage princess, must have made a wry face when she read this letter, but perhaps her sorrow was a little mitigated on learning that the Comte de Lauraguais was the son of the Duc de Villars Brancas, peer of France, Knight of the Golden Fleece, and Lieutenant General in the Army. If the young man only acted honourably, as he promised to do, Sophie might one day be a duchess.

The first lover of Sophie Arnould was not the sort of man to render her happy, for though he was not without some good qualities, he was jealous, passionate, eccentric and conceited.

Louis Léon Felicité, Comte de Lauraguais, and afterwards Duc de Brancas, was born in Paris, 3rd July, 1733, and died in that city October 9, 1824. At an early age he developed literary tastes, and when quite a youth wrote a tragedy. Concerning this production he told his friends that France hitherto had not possessed a real tragedy, but that he had remedied that deficiency. Actors and managers, however, did not appreciate the play, and he failed to get it produced. He next tried his hand at farce, and wrote the *Court of King Pétaud*

In this play there was a king who was dressed as a cook, with a white cap on his head, and a knife by his side. He has made some little tarts which he hands round to the courtiers who declare them super-excellent, divine, delicious. The only exception to this rule is one old courtier, who leans thought-fully against a chimney-piece and does not join in the general chorus of praise. King Pétaud asks him the meaning of this want of enthusiasm. "The tarts are excellent, no doubt, but, if I may speak without flattery," replies the courtier, "not so good as the woodcock pie which Your Majesty prepared the day before yesterday."

The King pats the old courtier on the back, and says, "That is right. I always like people to tell me the truth."

This farce was sent to the Italian comedians, but it is hardly necessary to say was refused. There-upon the Comte de Lauraguais read it to his father, the Duc de Brancas, stating that it was the work of a young man in whom he (Lauraguais) took an interest, and asked the Duc to exert his influence with the Minister to compel the comedians to accept the farce. The Duc declared that the play was an excellent one, and went off straight to the Minister, who was also pleased with the farce and at once dictated an order to the comedians to accept and produce *King Pétaud* without delay. Just as the order was about to be sent, a clerk, or some one

in the Minister's office, pointed out that His Majesty
Louis XV was also very fond of preparing dishes
with his own royal hands, and might therefore regard
the play as a personal insult, and if it were produced
the probable result would be that the theatre would
be shut up, the Minister would lose his place, and
the author and the Duc de Brancas would be sent
to the Bastille. It is needless to say that the
Minister, and the Duc were at once as anxious to
suppress the obnoxious farce as they had just been
to command its performance, and were ready to
curse their stupidity for not having seen the point
of the satire. *

In 1755—about three years before he made the
acquaintance of Sophie Arnould—the Comte de
Lauraguais married the Princesse d'Isingheim, who
seems to have been a good-hearted woman of a very
forgiving disposition, for she brought up two of the
illegimate children her husband had by the actress.

Not long after his elopement with Sophie Arnould,
the Comte de Lauraguais again came prominently
into public notice, but this time as a public reformer.
Up to that time it had been usual to allow gentlemen to occupy seats on the stage, which of course
interfered with the movements of the actors, and
utterly spoiled the effects of the finest scenes. The
absurdity of this arrangement had struck the actors
themselves, as well as all sensible persons in the

audience. The Comte de Lauraguais proposed to the actors of the Comédie Française that they should reconstruct the auditorium, and dispose, in the additional space thus gained, of the seats hitherto placed on the stage The actors were only too pleased to accede to this arrangement, but demurred to the cost of the alterations, which they estimated at 12,000 francs The Comte offered to pay the 12,000 francs out of his own pocket, and the 31st of March 1759, the workmen began the alterations On the 23rd of May the theatre re-opened, and the public warmly applauded the change in the appearance of the house. Grimm remarked that the change would not only compel the actors to provide more suitable scenery, but would create a revolution in "stage business," for the performers would no longer be compelled to stand in a circle like marionettes. * There was, however, a little wormwood in the cup, for when the bill for the alterations was presented, the amount was found to be 40,000 francs The actors endeavoured to prove that the alterations had been undertaken on the promise of Comte de Lauraguais to pay all the costs, but he replied that his liability only amounted to 12,000 francs, the estimated cost, that being all he had promised to pay. †

It somewhat detracted from the service he had been able to render the Comédie Française that he

* *Correspondance*, vol. iv page 111
† COLLE, *Journal et Mémoires* vol ii 170

expected a play of his to be acted at the theatre. From motives of gratitude the actors did not like to refuse, but the piece, which was a tragedy in three acts, and in prose, on the subject of *Iphigenia in Tauris*, was, if not bad, opposed to all the canons of the dramatic art then in force. "Luckily for himself," says Collé, "he withdrew it, for it was very bad. I was glad for his sake, though I do not know him." The same writer also recounts that de Lauraguais had at this time another tragedy ready, entitled *The Wrath of Achilles*. He read over this play to the Comte du Luc. "You must at least own," he said, as he folded up the manuscript at the conclusion of the reading, "that I have depicted the wrath of the hero very naturally."

"Oh, yes," replied du Luc, "you have made him as angry as a turkey-cock."

The elopement of Sophie Arnould with the Comte de Lauraguais was the talk of the town for some days, and much sympathy was expressed for the neglected wife. The Abbé Arnould took the Comte severely to task for his conduct, and the only defence de Lauraguais could make was to expatiate on the beauty, talent, and wit of his mistress.

"Have you quite finished?" said the Abbé at the close of this tirade "Now put public opinion into the other scale."

The Comte in his usual impulsive manner embraced the Abbé, and cried

"I am the happiest man in the world. I have a virtuous wife, a charming mistress, and a sincere friend."

The *liaison* was a tolerably long one considering that both parties were changeable, for Sophie Arnould had four children, three sons and a daughter, by her lover. They eventually grew tired of each other, but for the first two years they were a most loving couple. Sophie was hardly more than eighteen when she ran away from home, and if we may judge from her portrait by La Tour, a copy of which, engraved by Bourgeois de la Richardière, is prefixed to *Arnoldiana*, must have been exceedingly beautiful. The original portrait was executed in pastel— indeed La Tour never worked in anything else, as his nerves were so delicate that it made him ill to use colours mixed with oil. One good result of this ultra-sensitiveness was that he attained a wonderful grace and delicacy of execution in his own particular branch of art, and made the other artists so jealous of him that they refused to admit chalk drawings into the Salon Exhibition.

Sophie Arnould is depicted as singing, with the mouth half-open, and the large expressive eyes turned heavenward. The face is oval, and the features small and regular. The eyebrows are large and arched; the hair, which is abundant, appears to be powdered. From the inscription beneath the engraving we learn that she is represented in the

character of Psyché in the opera-ballet *Zehndor*. No
opera of that name is mentioned by Fétis, Campar-
don. Croyet, or Clement and Larousse, but it is
evidently the same work as *Zelie et Lindor*, which
is referred to by Grimm as a despicably bad and
worthless piece produced in 1763, and speedily
withdrawn. Sophie Arnould would then have been
twenty-three

The most complete pen-portrait we have of her
was written by Sophie Arnould herself, and, of
course, her testimony is not impartial. She says
that though her figure was small, it was lithe and
well formed, and her frame *(charpente)* graceful and
easy. " I have a well-made leg, pretty foot; hand
and arm like a model; well-shaped eyes, and a
frank, attractive, and intellectual face."

It will be seen that she had rather a good opinion
of herself, though it is but fair to say that La Tour's
portrait bears out the flattering description she gives
of her charms Grimm and Collé both speak of
her talent as being heightened by her youth and
beauty Mme. Vigée-Lebrun, however, says: "she
was not pretty, her mouth spoiled the beauty of her
face, but her eyes gave her a piquant look, and
were indicative of the wit which has made her
celebrated."

Against this consensus of opinion one or two
unfavourable opinions are to be placed. M. de
Sartines, the Lieutenant of the Police, employed

"inspectors" to write down all that went on in
Paris every day and send it to him. The reports
are not very interesting reading, and mainly consist
of items relating to the most notorious *cocottes* of
the day, such as, "The Russian Ambassador returned
to Paris yesterday and at once went to visit Mlle
A. at her lodgings in the Palais Royal; or "Comte
B. has discarded Mlle C. and taken Mlle D. of
the Opera for his mistress." From the close acquaintance shown with the doings of these damsels it is
natural to presume that if they did not write the
reports themselves they prompted the persons who
did. Many of these *demi-mondaines* had winced
under the satire of Sophie Arnould's sharp tongue,
and possibly used these reports as a means of
obtaining revenge. Perhaps this may account for
the very unflattering portrait of Mlle Arnould written
by one of M. de Sartines' inspectors. "I have
seen her getting out of bed. Her skin is black and
dry, and her mouth always full of saliva, so that
when she speaks you get all the cream of her
discourse in your face." *

M. de Goncourt regrets to find that this caricature
is confirmed by another writer, who says that "there
is nothing remarkable about her, her face is long
and thin, she has a villainously ugly mouth, large,
bared teeth, and a black and greasy skin." † It is

* *Documents inédits sur le règne de Louis XV.* Brussels 1863
† *L'Espion Anglais*, 1809

not impossible that both descriptions were written
by the same person, who was at the same time
a pamphleteer, police spy, and pimp. The discrepancy
as to the skin, which one says was *greasy*, may have
been due to a failure in memory, as it is not likely
that the inspector would have kept a copy of his
report.

From other accounts we learn that her teeth were
very bad and several of them so decayed that they
caused her breath to be offensive. Whether there
was any foundation for this statement it would be
difficult to say, but the science of dentistry was not
in a very advanced state in those days, and, if she
did suffer from this cause, would have found no
remedy except the radical one of having all the
teeth so affected, extracted.

M. de Sartines must have had sources of information
more trustworthy than those of the inspectors, or his
reputation for omniscience would rest on a very
slight basis. * Many of the items reported to him
are quite false. Sophie Arnould is painted as a
grasping, avaricious, and extravagant woman, who
in a few months cost her lover a hundred thousand
livres, and when she found that he was near the
bottom of his purse, left him for a richer admirer.

This does not accord with an anecdote related
by Diderot in his Memoirs, and which he heard,
he says, from the Abbé Raynal. Sophie Arnould

* *Life and Times of Madame du Barry*, by R. B. Douglas, page 52.

was one day in the company of some rich *demi-mondaine* who noticed that the actress wore no diamonds.

"Is it possible, Mademoiselle, that you have no diamonds," she cried

"No, Madam, nor do I think them necessary for a little *bourgeoise* of the Rue de la Tour."

"Ah, then I suppose you have a handsome allowance?"

"Why should I have an allowance? M. de Lauraguais has a wife and children, and a position to keep up, and I could not honestly accept a portion of a fortune which legitimately belongs to others."

Sophie's interlocutor was so astonished at this doctrine that she could only say:

"Well, if I were in your place I should leave him."

"That may be," replied Sophie, "but he likes me, and I like him. It may have been imprudent to take him, but as I have done so I shall keep him."

At all events Sophie did not pay her debts, for on 13th of November, 1759, Jean Baptiste Delamarre, *huissier*, acting on behalf of Jean Baptiste Desper, wigmaker, required the attendance of the commissaire of police to see an execution put in an apartment on the first floor at a certain house in the Rue de Richelieu. The said apartment had been leased for a term of three, six, or nine years, by the Demoiselle Arnould of the Opera, at a rent of 2400 livres per

annum. Nearly a year had expired, for the lease
was dated November 16, 1758, and wigmaker Desper
had not seen any of the rent. A levy was accordingly
made upon the goods of Mlle Arnould in the presence
of the commissaire of police, and the goods seized
were left in charge of a certain Sieur Chevalier,
a fruiterer.

The Opera did not make any heavy call on the
talents of Sophie Arnould for some time after the
production of *Enée et Lavinie*. The only other new
work brought out in the course of the year (1758)
was *Les Fêtes d'Euterpe*, an opera in four acts by
as many different writers, with music by the popular
composer of the day, d'Auvergne. Only one new
work, and that an unimportant one entitled *Fragments
héroïques* was produced in 1759, but early in 1760
(February 12th) a new opera called *Les Paladins* was
played for the first time. The music was by Rameau,
the greatest composer of whom France could boast
at that time. The libretto, which was by Monticour,
was poor, for Rameau cared very little for the words
he had to set to music. In fact at one of the
rehearsals of this particular opera Rameau repeatedly
told one of the actresses to take a certain air much
faster.

" But if I sing it so fast," said the *artiste*, " the
public will not be able to hear the words."

"That doesn't matter," replied the composer, " I
only want them to hear my music."

In spite of the reputation of Rameau, *Les Paladins* did not meet with any success, and was soon withdrawn—before the public had time to learn to appreciate the music, the composer declared; "The pear was not ripe," he said.

"That did not prevent it from falling all the same," retorted Sophie Arnould. [*]

Apart from the reputation which she enjoyed on the stage, Sophie Arnould was also making for herself a more lasting celebrity in the green-room When quite a child, she had, she says, striven to make clever remarks in order to attract the attention of the wits who sometimes visited her mother's house, and thus get praised for her precocity She soon noticed that the more biting a jest was the more successful it was, as evidenced by the mortification of the person at whom it was levelled, and the amusement of the other hearers. She therefore cultivated a caustic wit, and when she came out into the world she found plenty of objects for her satire. Many of her sharpest sallies were made at the expense of her fellow actresses, whose morals were no worse than her own, but she had, or affected to have, a cynical indifference as to her own reputation which effectually stopped all *tu quoque* retorts.

She soon became celebrated for her ready replies, and there were few wits of the time—though they were not deficient in number in the 18th century —

* The repartee is also ascribed to Mlle Carton

who cared to indulge in a contest of *persiflage* with her. Indeed so dreaded was her satire that people saw a veiled sarcasm even in her most innocent remark. Sydney Smith said that if he asked for the salt the whole table was in a roar, and whenever she opened her mouth in conversation, her hearers began to search for the sneer that was supposed to lurk within her words. She relates that the only time she ever saw Louis XV the King was at dinner. He was just raising a glass to his lips when she caught his eye. She said, almost involuntarily, "The King drinks." Louis blushed, put down his glass, and made a sign to one of the courtiers to lead her from the room.

In these pages we have endeavoured to give all her best witticisms, as they are recounted in the pages of *Arnoldiana*; the only ones omitted are those in which her wit is not up to its usual standard, or those which would not be to the taste of English readers.

Unfortunately it is not always possible to translate all her repartees. Many of them were puns; some puns upon names (which have been rightly considered as the lowest form of wit) and from some of those which are not puns, part of the spirit evaporates when they are rendered in another language. Some of her "good things" can be put into English with tolerable fidelity, though even then a reader who was conversant with both languages would probably agree with the celebrated wit, who said that "nothing except a Bishop was *improved* by translation "

The principal persons to suffer from Sophie Arnould's tongue were her fellow performers. Not one of them escaped her pitiless epigrams, and they had to bear them as best they could. One of them, a Mlle Peslin, angrily told Mlle Arnould never to mention her name again—"say nothing, either good or bad, about me."

"Ah, my dear," replied Sophie, "I am afraid I shall not be able to more than half obey you."

The two chief victims of Sophie's wit, at the outset of her dramatic career, were Mlle Beaumenard, and Mlle Guimard. The former was the mistress of a *fermier général* named d'Ogny, who had presented her with a magnificent *rivière* of diamonds. Some one was praising before Sophie Arnould this splendid necklace, but said that its only fault was that it was much too long and therefore fell too low over the wearer's figure.

" C'est qu'elle retourne vers sa source," said the witty actress.

This Mlle Beaumenard had, amongst her numerous lovers, a rich Englishman with whom she had quarrelled, and who came to Sophie Arnould to beg her to effect a reconciliation with his mistress.

"Let me first know the cause of the quarrel," said Sophie.

" Why, you know that she had a spaniel," answered

the Englishman, "and this little beast would come yapping round my heels; so one day I gave it a kick that unfortunately killed it However, to make up for it, I bought a beautiful little dog, and gave it to her, and she took the poor little thing and threw it through the window and it was killed on the pavement "

"Why your story is like a new version of the massacre of the innocents," said Sophie.

After ruining a whole host of rich lovers, Mlle Beaumenard married Belcourt, one of the actors at the theatre. Her charms had faded by that time, and she led a tolerably regular life after her marriage. Some one, alluding to her early career, said that she was then like a weather-cock, veering round to a fresh lover every day.

"Yes," answered the ever-ready Sophie, "and very like a weather-cock in this also, that she did not b come fixed till she was rusty."

Mlle Guimard, another butt for Sophie's wit, was a ballet-dancer. She was very tall and thin, and as many jokes were made about her long lean figure, as were made a few years ago about a great actress still living Sophie Arnould said that when she saw Mlle Guimard dancing a *pas de trois* with two male dancers, Gardel and Dauberval, it put her in mind of two dogs fighting for a bone.

Mlle Guimard was notorious for her gallantries, and when in the height of her notoriety possessed a magnificent hotel in the Chaussée d'Antin, on the spot now occupied by portion of the Opera house. She was extremely charitable, and good-hearted, but her good qualities did not save her from Sophie Arnould's sharp tongue. Perhaps Sophie was jealous of the rich lovers Mlle Guimard always had in her train. Mlle Guimard was more noted for statuesque beauty than for lightness and grace of movement, though she could not have been as awkward as Sophie pretended, for when a few years later, a piece of scenery fell on the *danseuse* and broke her arm, Mlle Arnould uncharitably said that "it was a great pity it was not her leg, for then she would not have been prevented from dancing."

It was not, however, only on her comrades that Sophie Arnould vented her wit. She had a sarcasm ready for every person whose name might happen to be mentioned in green-room gossip, and though not a hundredth part of her sayings have been preserved, they were no doubt duly repeated to the person who had been the object of her satire. A certain Duke, whose stupidity and conceit had often formed the subject of green-room jests, once accosted Sophie Arnould, and said:

"I hear, mademoiselle, that you pretend to be a wit, and make fun of your betters."

"*I* pretend to be a wit—" replied Sophie with affected simplicity. "I can assure you, monsieur, that I no more assume to be a wit than you do."

CHAPTER III.

*Comte de Lauraguais perpetrates a tragedy and takes it to Voltaire—
Sophie gets rid of her old lover, and takes a new one, then changes
back again — The Comte de Lauraguais prints his tragedy—Sophie's
stage successes— A pamphleteer of the Eighteenth Century — Sophie
cultivates the domestic virtues.*

(*1761—1762*)

THE irregular union subsisting between Sophie
Arnould and the Comte de Lauraguais had lasted
about three years, when it temporarily came to a
close in 1761. He was an impulsive, head-strong,
passionate man, with half a dozen hobbies which he
tried to ride all at once. The shortest and most
complete sketch of his character might be given by
quoting Dryden's famous lines on the Duke of
Buckingham from *Absalom and Achitophel*, for he
was a chemist of no mean acquirements, tried to
be a statesman, or at least a public reformer, and
dabbled in law, letters, medicine, and half a dozen
other subjects. Voltaire said of him : " He has all
possible talents, and all possible eccentricities, with
more wit and knowledge than any man of his kind." *
His violent advocacy of his own views, and hearty

Letter 30th Sept 1761. Works vol. XLI, p 464

abuse of everybody who did not happen to agree
with him, brought him into constant trouble with
the authorities, and he was exiled five times, and
clapped in prison four times. It should be added
that neither punishment induced him to alter his
opinions. A story is told of him that on his
reappearance at Court after one of these short terms
of exile, Louis XV asked him what he had done
in England

"Sire," replied de Lauraguais coldly, "j'ai appris
à *penser.*"

"Des chevaux?" asked the King quickly *

Sophie Arnould was not happy with such a lover.
She said in after years, that he had given her two
million kisses, and cost her four million tears. Nor
does she appear to have had any great affection for
the children she bore him. A characteristic anecdote
is related of her concerning the birth of her first
child. A few days after this event, several of her
female friends and stage comrades called on her,
and she was giving them a graphic description of the
pains of childbirth when her doctor, who was in
the room, interrupted her.

"There is a very simple way of preventing all this
pain," he said gravely.

* This incident, though inserted here to illustrate the character of de
Lauraguais, occurred several years later than the time of which we are now
writing The point of the retort lies in the similarity of pronunciation of
penser and *panser*. *Panser un cheval* means " to groom or rub down a
horse."

"And what is that?" asked Sophie

"Chastity!" he replied.

"Ah, doctor," said Sophie with a merry laugh; "the remedy is worse than the complaint."

In spite of the ties between them, Sophie Arnould was only seeking a pretext to get rid of her lover, and a favourable opportunity soon occurred.

The Comte de Lauraguais had "perpetrated" a tragedy in five acts, on the not very novel subject of Clytemnestra. He had dedicated this work, long before its completion, to Voltaire, and as soon as he had finished it, determined to take it to the Master, and perhaps get one or two hints from the more experienced playwright. He left Paris for Ferney some time in September of this year (1761), for Voltaire writing to the Comtesse de Lutzelbourg under date of 30th September, says "I have now staying with me the greatest chemist in France, who no doubt will make me young again: it is the Comte de Lauraguais." *

Before his departure the Comte had requested his friend, M. Berton, to look after Sophie during his absence. Berton was *trésorier des parties casuelles* to the King, and a very rich man. It is possible that his riches had quite as much to do with Sophie's resolve as the bad temper of her old lover, but at any rate, as soon as she was sure that he had arrived at Geneva, she placed in the carriage that

* *Voltaire, Complete Works,* vol. XLI, p. 464.

he had given her, all the presents she had ever received from him, and also the two children she had borne him, and sent the whole equipage to the Hotel de Lauraguais.

At the same time she sent off to the Comte the following letter.

"My dear friend,

You have written a tragedy which is so fine that I do not understand it any more than your other proceedings. You have left for Geneva, in order to receive a wreath of the laurels of Parnassus from M. de Voltaire, and I am alone and deserted. I have taken advantage of my liberty—liberty that is so dear to philosophers—to leave you. Do not think this wrong or cruel of me, I am tired of a lover who is a madman,—who has dissected his coachman, and who wished to act as my *accoucheur*, —no doubt with the intention of dissecting me. Allow me therefore to remove myself out of the reach of your philosophic bistoury."

Having sent this letter she very wisely put herself under the protection of the police, for she knew the violence of de Lauraguais' character. When he received this epistle and read it he clutched his valet by the shoulder, and cried, "Support me, Fabian, for the blow is more than I can bear."

He posted off at once to Paris, and tried by entreaties, threats, and other means to persuade his mistress to return to him, but though he "vomited

fire and flames," Sophie was not to be persuaded,
—for some months at least. *

She had also the advantage of having got rid of
the children, for Madame de Lauraguais returned
the carriage and the jewels which Sophie had sent
back, but adopted the two illegitimate sons of her
husband

M. Bertin, who had become the protector of
Sophie, *vice* de Lauraguais deposed, provided for
his mistress a richly furnished apartment, and one
of de Sartines' inspectors, writing under date of 20th
November, says he can make a very good guess
as to the ultimate destination of a fine carriage which
had been ordered by M. Bertin from a tradesman
of the singular name of Antechrist.

An equipage of this sort was almost a necessity for
a kept woman of any notoriety, and there was no
nymph of the Opera with any self-respect who could
exist without a carriage and pair One of the ladies
of the ballet, Mlle Grandi, said one night, in the
green-room of the Opera, that all she wanted to
make her supremely happy was a carriage and pair,
and an income of 100,000 francs or so in order
to enable her to live up to the carriage. The next
day there arrived at her house a magnificent chariot
drawn by four horses. The donor of this handsome

---

* The story is taken from Favart's *Mémoirs*, and though correct as to the
main facts, there is reason to believe that he invented the letter we have
quoted

gift did not present himself at the time, and that night at the Opera Mlle Grandi boasted about her present, and wondered if her unknown lover was old or young, handsome or ugly.

"My dear Grandi," said Sophie Arnould, "presents of that sort fall from the sky, and therefore it must be an angel who sends them."

As a matter of fact the equipage came from a tradesman who had never been paid for it, and had been ordered by a Polish *chevalier d'industrie* who in return for his supposed gift enjoyed the favours of the *danseuse* for a few days, and then disappeared. The carriage-builder, who had found out the destination of the carriage, called upon Mlle Grandi to ask to whom he was to look for his money, but before he could say a word, she began to find fault with the horses' paces—for it seems to have been usual at that time for the *sellier* to supply the horses as well as the carriage. The wily tradesman assured her that that was the fault of the coachman, and that if *he* drove she would have no cause to be dissatisfied. Mlle Grandi thereupon ordered out the carriage; stepped into it, and the *sellier* mounted the box. On arriving on the Boulevards he told her he was going to make the horses caracole, and as there might be danger she had better get out for a minute or two. She did so, and he at once whipped up the team and drove them back to his stables, leaving the lady standing disconsolate on the pavement.

Bertin sent a letter to the Comte de Lauraguais to say that he intended to take Sophie for his mistress, for in the 18th Century there was an etiquette to be observed in these matters. The Comte took what he doubtless considered to be a very neat revenge by becoming the protector of Mlle Hus, the actress who had just thrown over Bertin.

Sophie's new lover was a dull, heavy man, a mere plutocrat, and he could find no better method to gain the affection, or secure the fidelity of his mistress, than to load her with gifts. By the end of the year he had expended 100,000 francs upon her, exclusive of a sum of 12,000 francs for her New Year's gift But love for Lauraguais still smouldered in her breast, and almost on the very day that she received this last present she showed Bertin the door, and invited back her old lover, who was not loth to come.

To the unprejudiced English reader, Sophie Arnould's conduct on this occasion must seem singularly heartless, unprincipled, and venal, but to the Frenchmen of those days it appeared little short of heroic. Bachaumont,—who, fortunately for the present writer, begins what Carlyle calls his "thirty volumes of scurrilous eaves-dropping" on 1st January 1762— records the incident almost on his first page, and grows quite snively about it. All Paris, he says, was discussing the conduct of two lovers who had mutually agreed to forget each others' faults, and had displayed a constancy worthy of the days of old.

Less than three weeks later Bachaumont does not see quite so much to admire in the reconciliation between Sophie and the Comte de Lauraguais, and records that people were beginning to say that Bertin had been hardly treated. If the transaction is to preserve a heroic character, he says, then the favoured lover must pay back to the rejected one, the very large sums which the latter had expended on his unfaithful mistress, but as that has not been done, he (Bachaumont) is of opinion that Mlle Arnould has gained the admiration of tender and susceptible hearts under false pretences, and she must therefore —morally at least—"be relegated to the crowd of women from which she has been drawn." Bachaumont's indignation seems to have been a trifle premature, for there is no doubt that Comte de Lauraguais did indemnify his less lucky rival, and that Bertin "lost nothing, except the most charming woman in Paris." *

This second disappointment threw him into a state of grief which provoked the pity of the Parisians. Sophie overheard at the Comédie Française, only a few days after she had left the financier, two young men conversing, and saying what a shame it was that a man so rich, easy-going, generous, good, sensible, and amiable as Bertin, should have met with such an ungrateful and faithless mistress.

* Emile Gaboriau, *Les Comédiennes adorées*, p. 29

She turned away impatiently, saying as she did so,
"On voit bien que ces messieurs ne l'ont pas eu."

Perhaps she did not feel quite sure that she might
not be hissed if she appeared at the theatre, for
she did not sing again until Feb. 18th, when she
played the small but effective part of *Psyché* in
l'Amour et Psyché. The public had forgiven her,
and the applause when she came on the stage was
indescribable * The *Mercure de France* is not quite
so complimentary and remarks that she has lost
nothing of what voice she had, and that if the tune
rather dragged in her songs that was doubtless owing
to nervousness or emotion.

This same month the Comte de Lauraguais printed
his tragedy of *Clytemnestra*, which the actors of the
Comédie Française had refused to play. Their
refusal was justifiable, for the Comte de Ségur, to
whom de Lauraguais read his tragedy, declared at
the end of the reading that the only three verses
he had understood were those uttered by the Sphynx!
—a criticism at which the author was indignant. †
Bad as the tragedy undoubtedly was, it was perhaps
not so bad as that, but de Lauraguais being a very
passionate man his acquaintances loved to tease him.
On another occasion Comte de Ségur and the Chevalier de Boufflers asked de Lauraguais to explain
to them a book called *Des erreurs de la Vérité*,—

Bachaumont, *Mémoires secrets*, vol 1, p 48
r Comte de Ségur, Memoires vol 1, p 150

a philosophical work which was then being much discussed in Paris. De Lauraguais complied, and when he had expounded the doctrines of the book for two hours or so, his friends stopped him. Before he began, they said, they had been able to gather some meaning in an occasional sentence in the book, but now they understood absolutely nothing about it.

In May, Sophie appeared as *Cleopatra* in one of those curious productions peculiar to the time, of which we have already spoken,—four or five one act operas having no connection with each other, and each having its separate ballet. Her friends, Bachaumont says, had disgusted her with the part and told her that it was unworthy of her great talents, so she refused to play it, until she was threatened with imprisonment if she did not, but " her acting seemed constrained and unnatural " to Bachaumont, though the critic of the *Mercure de France*, being probably unacquainted with the cabals of the *coulisses*, thought her interesting figure, and the charms of her singing and acting, lent fresh charms .to the piece;—a proof that even then critics saw exactly what they expected to see. In this instance Bachaumont was most likely right, for after a few representations the part was made over to Mlle Hebert,— a *débutante* who is spoken of as a very tall but well-proportioned young woman.

For the next few months Sophie Arnould appears to have led a very quiet life. She did not sing in

.

public and her private life was dull and uneventful.
This would hardly have been the case if she had
still been under the protection of the Comte de
Lauraguais, but these curious lovers were like magnets,
true to a common ideal so long as they were separate, but mutually repelling each other when they
came together.

The reports which were brought in by the spies
of Mr. de Sartines were intended to afford information
to the Lieutenant of Police, and amusement to the
King. Louis XV. would send half a dozen times
in the course of a morning to know whether the
police reports had arrived, and as soon as they
came to hand lost no time in perusing them. The
astute Lieutenant had of course informed his subor-
dinates as to the kind of items the King preferred,
and they carefully recorded how many times a
leading demi-mondaine changed her "protector,"
what jewellery she received; how many hours a
certain ambassador's carriage stood at the door of
a certain actress; and other details of a like nature.
It is not improbable that some of the scandal inserted
in these reports was invented by the imaginative
spies in the pay of Mr. de Sartines. One of the
cleverest of the scoundrels who was in the pay of
the police,- Chevrier,—died this year. He had
libelled some person of quality who had thereupon
announced that his valets carried cudgels, and had
orders to thrash Chevrier on sight, and Chevrier

deemed it advisable to leave France. He went to Holland where he died, most probably of starvation, but his friends—if he can be said to have had any —set it abroad that he had been poisoned.

"Poisoned!" cried Sophie Arnould, when she heard the rumour, "—then he must have sucked his own pen."

At this particular time the spies could find little to say about Sophie, and nothing to say against her. They report that she was often to be seen walking in the Tuileries Gardens, accompanied by her mother and her sister, and so plainly dressed that she passed for a *petite bourgeoise*. Sometimes she was leaning on the arm of a good-looking young man who was said to be her hair-dresser, which caused the report to be circulated that she was about to marry him. The report reached M. de Saint Florentin, the Minister, who twitted the actress about it on the next occasion on which she paid an official visit to him, but, "with some difficulty, she persuaded him that there was no truth in the rumour."

In the society of her family, her hair-dresser, and possibly sometimes de Lauraguais,—for these extraordinary lovers appear to have been always meeting, quarrelling, and parting again,—Mlle Arnould passed the summer of 1762. On October 12th, she again appeared at the theatre, this time in the Opera of *Alphée et Aréthuse*. According to the few critics of that day, her return to the stage was welcomed

with delight by the audience.   Whether her comrades
of the theatre were quite as pleased to have her
back amongst them may reasonably be doubted,
but she appears to have put a curb upon her tongue,
for of the many satirical things she uttered, none
can be referred to this period.

CHAPTER IV.

A new stage-effect—The Opera-house destroyed by fire—The origin of two theatrical terms—De Lauraguais writes about Inoculation, and is sent to prison in consequence—Sophie sings before the King—She successfully appeals for her lover's release—The Comtesse de Lauraguais retires to a convent—Sophie Arnould's children—Sophie and the Lieutenant of Police—Poinsinet the poet—Some of the practical jokes played upon him—Death of Rameau.

(1763—1764)

IN January 1763, Mlle Arnould scored another triumph in a new opera which the *Mercure de France* calls *Polixène*, but the full title of which was *Pyrrhus et Polixène*, the music being by M. d'Auvergne, and the words by M. Joliveau, " Perpetual Secretary of the Royal Academy of Music." Her voice appeared to have improved, but perhaps the critics were inclined to be lenient, as they were in raptures over a new stage-effect which was first introduced at the production of this opera. The " back-cloth " was usually painted to represent a sunny sky, that being the most suitable for ordinary circumstances, but when storms were required, " the horizon being fixed " never showed anything but a pure and serene sky. The scenic artist, M. Girault, hit upon the plan of making the cloth double the length and fastening the top and bottom to rollers. The lower part was painted with dark clouds which were rolled up or down as required:—a device which appears now extremely simple, but was then considered as an enormous advance in scenic art.

Towards the end of the same month she also sang before the King and Court, at Versailles, and, as usual, took part in the Sacred Concerts, which were given in the beginning of Lent.

On the morning of April 6th, 1763, the workmen engaged at the Opera, found that the theatre was on fire. Instead of at once calling for assistance, they endeavoured to put it out themselves, and for two or three hours they managed to prevent the flames from spreading. About eleven o'clock the fire suddenly increased, and the alarm was then given, but it was too late. Two thousand persons, including a number of monks and nuns, helped to pass buckets of water, but that primitive method of extinguishing a conflagration was not likely to prove very successful with a burning theatre, and by half-past twelve the building was completely gutted.

The loss of the Opera does not appear to have greatly grieved the Parisians. Plenty of epigrams were made about it, but most of them are now forgotten. There was not a good supply of water handy at the beginning of the fire, and some one accounts for this by saying that no one had expected a fire to break out in an ice-house. Favart, who was interested in the Italian Opera, expressed a wish that all French music might perish along with the Opera house; and the Abbé Galiani, whose reputation as a wit appears to have been easily acquired, if we may judge by the specimens which have come down to us, suggested that the new Opera-house should be erected at the Sèvres barrier, opposite the arena where bull-fights were held, as " all loud noises should be outside the city." *

That would hardly have suited the pocket of the Duc d'Orléans, who long before the rafters had done smoking, had obtained from the King permission to build a larger and finer theatre on the same site. Louis XV was also pleased to order that the Salle des Machines in the Tuileries Palace should be used as a theatre in the meantime, that his good people of Paris should not be deprived of an amusement of which they were so fond. It took several months to prepare the building, for it was not till January 24th, 1764, that the first performance took place there, when *Castor et Pollux* was played. The Salle des Machines was not a very comfortable theatre, but it has left a record of itself in one of the commonest terms of the French stage, the origin of which is not generally known. In English theatres the prompter usually stands at the wing to the right hand of the

* *Correspondance*, de Grimm, Diderot, etc Vol V p. 271.

spectators and that side of the stage is known as
the "prompt side," and the other as "opposite
prompt," or—more briefly as P. S. and O. P.
respectively. In France, where the prompter's box
is in the centre of the stage on a level with the
foot-lights, this method of nomenclature could not be
adopted, but as it was usual for the King and Queen,
whenever they visited the theatre, to have separate
boxes facing each other, the different sides of the
stage were known to the actors as the King's side
or Queen's side. These terms lasted down to the
Revolution, when of course they were abolished as
savouring too much of royalty, but it was not easy
to discover another expression to take their
place An actor remembered that in the old
Salle des Machines the court was one side and the
garden on the other, and the terms "Cour" and
"Jardin" are still daily used by every French
actor.

Whether Sophie Arnould and the Comte de
Lauraguais had once more come together at this
time it would be difficult to say, for they were always
mutually attracting and repelling each other, but if
so, they were about to be ruthlessly separated for
some months at least.

Inoculation for the small-pox had, as every school-
boy knows, been introduced into England by Lady
Mary Wortley Montague early in the 18th Century,
but though Voltaire as early as 1727 had warmly

advocated the practice, * and had been seconded by
Jean Jacques Rousseau, the French were unwilling
"to incur a certain danger in order to escape an
uncertain risk," and inoculation was still practically
unknown in France. Perhaps when the Comte went
to Ferney to show his tragedy to Voltaire, the old
philosopher had mentioned the subject, for soon after
his return to Paris, de Lauraguais wrote a *Mémoire
sur l'inoculation* As was usual with him, in this
pamphlet he heartily abused every one who did not
agree with him, including not only the doctors—
which would not have mattered much,—but also the
magistrates. He read this pamphlet at the Academy
of Sciences, of which he was a member

In those days it was dangerous to speak one's
mind too freely, and de Lauraguais was arrested
and sent to Metz. He was locked up in the citadel,
and kept there for six months. He employed his
leisure in bombarding the Minister with long testimonials or laudatory letters about the Commandant
of the citadel, whose harshness and cruelty, he said,
made him a model gaoler who deserved promoting
to the governorship of a large prison. With most
men we should have no hesitation in saying that
these testimonials were "rit sarkastik," but the Comte
was such an extraordinary character that there is a
great probability he was serious.

* *Lettres Philosophiques* No XI Works (Edition Delangle) Vol XXXV
page 75 *et seq.*

His wife—that much-enduring and much-forgiving
woman,—and his friends, did all they could to procure his release, but the Duc de Choiseul was not
to be moved. An appeal to Louis XV was not
likely to prove successful for the Comte was in the
King's "black books," and perhaps more than
usually so, on account of a remark he had let
drop at the time of his arrest. Before starting for
Metz, de Lauraguais had requested to be taken to
Versailles in order that he might see the King.
On arriving at the Palace, de Lauraguais was
informed that the King was out hunting. "Well,"
he said coolly, "cannot he be arrested by a
lettre de cachet."

The *artistes* of the Opera, having no theatre in
Paris at which they could perform, played several
times before the Court. In November the old opera
of *Dardanus* was given with Sophie Arnould in the
part of *Iphise* the heroine. Her performances were
always remarkable for dramatic force and on this
occasion she surpassed herself, and even succeeded
in dissipating the King's *ennui* for an hour or two.
Taking advantage of the sensation she had created,
she threw herself at the feet of the Duc de Choiseul
and implored him, in the name of *Iphise* to release
"her *Dardanus.*" The Duc was perfectly well aware
that *Dardanus* was the Comte de Lauraguais, and
granted Sophie's request, but, on condition, Bachaumont declares, that there should be a separation

between the Comte and Comtesse.* It is doubtful
whether Choiseul ever made such a proposition, but
the ill-assorted pair were separated shortly after.
The Comte de Lauraguais as soon as he was released
rushed back to Paris, threw himself into the arms
of Sophie Arnould, declared that she was his deliverer
and that he would never leave her, and refused to
see his wife. This was too much for the patience
of the Comtesse and she soon afterwards obtained
a separation. Perhaps she derived some satisfaction
from learning during the course of the next few
years that he was no more faithful to any of his
many mistresses than he had been to his wife.

With the exception of these performances at Court,
the only opportunities which the *artistes* had of being
heard, were at the Sacred Concerts. At these,
Sophie Arnould, according to the contemporary
critics, was excelled by none of her rivals. Her
beautiful face appeared to be illuminated by a deeply
religious fervour, and she threw so much intensity
and expression into an aria as almost to draw tears
from her auditors. But when once she was off the
platform she was quite a different person, and was
ready to crack a joke or utter a sarcasm whenever
the chance occurred. It was at one of these concerts
that a lady came and sat next the actress, and greatly
admired her beauty and her dress. When Sophie
rose to go on the platform, the lady discovered that

* *Mémoires secrets,* 24 Nov. 1763

her neighbour was not a *grande dame* of the Court,
but the somewhat notorious Mlle Arnould, of the
Opera. Hastily gathering up her skirts, lest they
should come into contact with the singer's robe, she
audibly remarked, that "it was a pity there was not
some distinguishing mark by which honest women
could be known from the strumpets."

Sophie turned upon her with a sweet smile, and
said, "Why, madam, should you wish to put the
filles to the trouble of counting the honest women?"

But her satire was not always so neat as this,
and her jokes were often but puns on the names of
persons,—and very poor puns too. It was at one
of these concerts that some one knocked down and
smashed the only harp in the orchestra, and the
concert had to be suspended until a fresh harp was
obtained, there being a solo passage for that instrument in the symphony about to be performed.
Mlle Arnould thereupon cried, "If you wish to be
in harmony, don't fetch *la Harpe* from Fort l'Evêque."

The allusion was to La Harpe,—a tolerably prolific but now almost forgotten tragedian,—who was
then a young man at college, and had been sent
to the prison of Fort l'Evêque for having written a
satire on his professors.

At the Sacred Concerts this year (1763) a Signor
Rhodolphe astonished all Paris by a wonderful performance upon the *cor de chasse* for with that un-
satisfactory instrument "he had attained such a degree

of perfection that he could imitate, by turns, the softest flute and the loudest trumpet." A musician who was jealous of the skilful performer said that a *cor de chasse* was not capable of expressing any tender sentiment or feeling. "To hear you talk," exclaimed Sophie Arnould, "one would imagine that Rhodolphe was *un cor sans âme.*"

The Comtesse de Lauraguais having retired to a convent *, there was nothing to interfere with the happiness of Sophie and her lover, but it was impossible for the Comte to remain faithful to any woman for any length of time,—indeed his eccentricities without his infidelities would have alone sufficed to disgust most women. Perhaps six months in the citadel of Metz had somewhat calmed down the exuberance of his spirits, and their irregular union was for three or four years unbroken, except by the short but rather frequent spells of exile which the Comte had to undergo.

The Comte's gratitude for his release caused him —we may infer—to devote the whole of such affection as he was capable of to Sophie. She bore him a son in the following October (1764), being the third son with which she had presented him. The child was baptised at the Church of St. Roch, and in the original entry in the register the words

* A MS volume of *Nouvelles à la main* in the Mazarin Library, Paris, is the only authority for this, but as no further mention of her occurs in any of the Memoirs, it seems likely that the statement is correct.

" father unknown " were inserted—from force of habit, no doubt—but Sophie Arnould afterwards obtained permission to "amend the record," and the name of the Comte de Lauraguais was then written.

It would perhaps be advisable to say a few words here regarding Sophie Arnould's children. Messrs. de Goncourt make a very singular mistake regarding the number of her sons,—an error which a very little care in revising would have obviated, and which is the more singular as in the biographical sketch prefixed to " Arnoldiana"—a book from which they constantly quote,—the names of all the children of Sophie Arnould are given in full. In the life by the de Goncourts it is stated that Mlle Arnould had two sons and a daughter, and they give extracts from baptismal registers showing that the younger boy was born in October 1764. They evidently overlooked the fact that they had stated but a few pages before that " one fine morning in 1761 Sophie sent to the Comte's hotel all the presents she had received from him, and also his two children!"

The two children sent in 1761 to the Comtesse de Lauraguais, and adopted by her, were Louis Dorval, born 1758, and Auguste Camille. The latter could not have been more than five or six weeks old, for he was born 27th August, 1761. The elder boy, Louis Dorval, died in 1762, aged four. As his young life came to such a premature conclusion, perhaps Messrs. de Goncourt did not think

him worth mentioning. How the younger boy was
brought up we cannot say. It is very probable that
the Comtesse de Lauraguais placed him with some
respectable people, and paid for his maintenance.
We hear little of him till he was grown up, when
we find both sons asking their mother for money
at a time she could ill afford it.

The third son Antoine Constant, born October 16th,
1764, was at first intended for the Church. He
afterwards changed his mind, and wanted to go to
England to prepare himself for a commercial career, but as his mother could not afford the money
for this, he went into the Army. He rose to be
Colonel of a Regiment of Cuirassiers, and was killed
whilst charging at the head of his men at the battle
of Wagram.

The youngest child and only daughter of Sophie
Arnould was Alexandrine Sophie, born March 7th,
1767. Some doubt might not unreasonably be
entertained as to her father, and it is said that
Sophie Arnould tried to persuade the Prince de
Conti that the paternity of the child was ascribable
to him. As that not-otherwise-distinguished nobleman had sixty recognised mistresses, without counting the "minor" and the "imperceptible" ones, she
doubtless thought that one illegitimate child more
or less made little difference. But according to
other accounts she was satisfied with making de
Lauraguais recognise the child and provide for its

future,— which he did by a deed dated 9th July
1768. Of Alexandrine Sophie — *filia digna*—more
will be said in due course.

The temporary theatre in the Salle des Machines
was ready in the beginning of 1764, and the first
performance was given on 24th January, when an
old opera entitled *Castor et Pollux* was played,
with Mlle Arnould as "*Zelaire*, the sister and
daughter of the Sun." The theatre, as we have said,
was not a comfortable or convenient one,—Sophie
called it "an ointment for a burn,"—and there is
reason to believe that the acoustic properties were
not very good; and as her voice was never over-
strong, this may account for the fact that she did
not sing very often during the six years that the
new opera house was in building. The surmise
may not be correct, for the critic of the *Mercure
de France* declares that on this opening-night,
" the interesting Mlle Arnould had never been seen
to greater advantage," and he credits her, not only
with grace, feeling, intelligence and other stage-
virtues, but says that in this new theatre her voice
had " more force, volume and roundness than it had
ever had before." Not only the sounds of her voice,
but the words, could be heard in every part of the
house, but this last effect, he is careful to add, is
doubtless the result of her faultless articulation.

A more probable reason for the rare appearance

of the name of Mlle Arnould on the play-bill is
that—at all events during the latter part of the six
years—she was spending all her time in dissipation
and vice, and cared very little for stage successes.
She infinitely preferred a supper-party with a score or
so of dissolute women and depraved men, but at
least there was no hypocrisy about her vice. She
never attempted to make herself out better than she
was, and she fearlessly satirized any of her companions
who assumed an affectation of virtue.

It was most likely about this time that she so
boldly and impudently answered M. de Sartines, the
Lieutenant of Police. A report reached the Lieutenant
of Police that at a supper-party given at Sophie
Arnould's house, some lampoons on Mme. de Pompadour had been sung or recited. The King's
mistress was a revengeful woman, and perhaps the
knowledge that she was rapidly dying made her
more ill-tempered than usual. In more than one
instance the not very heinous offence of writing or
singing a few scurrilous words about the favourite
had been punished by twenty years imprisonment
or even more. But it would have required more
than the fear of the Bastille to have prevented
Sophie Arnould from saying a good thing about de
Pompadour or anybody else, if the chance occurred,
and the Comte de Lauraguais, who was always to
be found amongst the ranks of the discontented, is
pretty sure to have cordially hated the royal mistress.

At all events,—if the story be true,—de Sartines called upon the actress one morning and the following dialogue ensued.

" Mademoiselle, where did you sup last night?"

" I do not remember."

" You supped at home."

" Very possibly "

" You had company."

" Most likely."

" Amongst your guests were some persons of high rank."

" That does happen sometimes."

" Who were those persons? "

" I do not remember."

" You do not remember the names of the persons who supped with you last night?"

" No, sir."

" But it seems to me that a woman like you ought to remember things of that sort."

" Yes," replied Sophie, " but before a man like you I am not a woman like me."

Thereupon the Lieutenant of Police walked away crest-fallen, having failed in his endeavour to make Sophie incriminate her guests, [k] or rather having failed to make her confirm the information his spies had given him, for, if the stories told about him are

This reply procured the actress twenty-four hours' imprisonment How she met in old man there who was imprisoned for debt, and how she procured his release by getting up a sham raffle for a gold chain which did not exist will be mentioned in another place

true, he had brought the police system to such perfection that very little went on in Paris that was not immediately made known to him. *

On 7th April, 1764, *Psyché* was revived at the Opera, with Mlle Arnould in the title *rôle*, and made such an impression on the susceptible critic of the *Mercure* that he declared that her acting and singing showed that "she had been far from perfection in those days when he had been the most enchanted with her,"—apparently meaning that she now eclipsed all her former performances. Having rendered "this praise, or rather this justice, to the charm of her talent," he goes on to say that praise is also due to her for never having broken faith with the public since the new theatre had been opened, and he hopes that the state of her health will permit her to continue this laudable "habitual exactness." In this, however, he was doomed to disappointment, for, a few nights later, she quitted the theatre, and did not re-appear for nearly a year.

The birth of her third son in October of this year will, to a great extent, account for this prolonged absence, but not entirely so, for she did not appear again till March 22nd, 1765. Whether she passed all this period in domestic peace and quietness with Comte de Lauraguais is doubtful, but nothing definite is known on the subject. Most probably the sarcastic

* Some instances of this acroamatic information have been already given in the *Life and Times of Madame du Barry*.

remark she made concerning Mlle Fel would have equally applied to herself. This actress had left the stage in 1758, and for several years had been living in retirement Some one was speaking of the quiet and virtuous life that Mlle Fel was leading, when Sophie cried, "Don't you trust her too much : she is like Penelope and undoes by night all that she has done by day." There was certainly no fear of Sophie giving up the vanities and vices of the world and living a secluded life, or becoming a nun, one of those women of whom she said, "They give themselves to God when the devil will no longer have them."

In all probability she aped the manners of the great ladies of the Court, who, if they were her superiors in birth, were her inferiors in wit, and her equals in morals That is to say she spent the morning in bed, or, if visitors arrived, reclined upon a couch, and sipped her chocolate, or toyed with her lap-dog, whilst poetasters like Poinsinet, and Dorat read her the verses they had composed in her honour, or abbés, of the Voisenon type, related all the latest scandal to her, and treasured up the sarcastic remarks she made thereon, that they might retail them elsewhere as their own. We can imagine her listening with amusement whilst de Lauraguais expounded some half-wise, half-foolish scheme; or shrinking from him in terror when he went into one of his ungovernable fits of passion and broke a

few thousand francs worth of furniture. But it is
difficult to think of her as passing whole mornings
under the hands of the *coiffeur* and the tire-woman,
or simpering over the platitudes of the house-poet
for the time being, or consulting some fledgling
abbé on the cut of a gown or the design of a
brocade. It is much more likely that the young
abbés went away doubting sorely whether the bright
eyes of the pretty actress altogether compensated
for her sharp tongue; and if the verses were bad,
—and judging from the few specimens which have
been preserved they were usually *very* bad,—the
author was informed of the fact with a frankness
that was not rendered the more pleasant by the
sarcasm with which it was mingled.

Poinsinet more than once was the object of these
not very flattering criticisms. He always brought
verses with him when he came to Sophie Arnould's
reception, and with these productions, "he imagined
he amused the company." Sophie, remarking the
soporific effect the lines had on the hearers, said,
"Poinsinet's verses are like spoiled children, their
father is the only person who likes them."

On one occasion the poet found a champion who
was bold enough to say that few authors had as
much wit as Poinsinet, to which Sophie Arnould
replied, "Poinsinet has so much wit in his head
that there is no room for common-sense," —which
does not appear to be a very original remark, but

5

was certainly true, for poor Poinsinet was the most
credulous of mortals, and was the butt for endless
practical jokes, few of which were clever and many
were cruel. At one time he was persuaded that
he was about to be appointed "screen-holder" to
the King, and every day for a fortnight was made
to stand, for some hours at a stretch, scorching his
legs in front of a large fire in order that he might
get accustomed to his duties. On another occasion
he was told that the Empress of Russia had promised to make him a member of the Academy of
St. Petersburg if he would learn Russian. A pro-
fessor was found for him, and for six months
Poinsinet studied hard, and then discovered that the
language he had been learning was not Russian at
all, but the Celtic dialect of Lower Brittany. He
had no sooner got over this disappointment than
he heard from a friend that the King of Prussia
would appoint him tutor to his son, if he would
first abjure the Catholic religion. An accomplice,
who was in the joke, pretended to be a chaplain of
the King, and to have come to France at the peril
of his life in order to initiate the poet in the tenets
of Lutheranism, and the victim was led into all
sorts of remote and secluded spots where the
religious instruction, or the nonsense that passed for
it, could be given without fear of detection.

When Poinsinet at last found out the truth he
wanted to charge his persecutors with conspiracy,

and was with difficulty persuaded by his *real* friends
that the laugh would be against him. He therefore
contented himself with calling out one of the conspirators. A duel was arranged, the parties met,
and at the first pass Poinsinet made, his adversary
fell, apparently wounded. Poinsinet was at once
hurried from the field, and a little later, he was
informed that he had killed his man, and had better
keep quietly at home for a short time. A few days
later he heard his name loudly bawled under his
windows, and peeping out saw a hawker who was
selling broad-sheets, and was calling out, "Poinsinet
condemned to be hanged for having killed a man."
The poor poet sent his servant for one of the
broad-sheets, and there was the horrible news confirmed in print. At this juncture a "friend" arrived,
and, of course, proffered his advice as to the best
course to be taken. It was that a barber should
be sent for and a tonsure shaved on Poinsinet's
head, and the supposed murderer could then don
the dress of an abbé, and make his escape from
Paris. The innocent victim of these relentless tor-
mentors consented, was got safely out of Paris, and
lurked in all sorts of hiding places, and was made
to assume all sorts of disguises, until the jokers
tired of the sport (!) and informed their cully that
the King had, out of admiration for his verses,
granted him a free pardon.

The excessive fatuity of this egregious *gobe-mouche*

here stood him in good stead, for he wrote to thank the King for his clemency. Louis XV was naturally puzzled, as he had never heard of the death of Poinsinet's adversary,—who, it is needless to say, was unhurt,—or of the sentence on the luckless poet. When the King did at last understand the affair he was indignant at finding that his name and the royal prerogative had been so freely used for the purpose of a practical joke, and the perpetrators of the hoax received a severe "wigging,"—which was considerably less than they deserved. Practical jokes are usually devoid of humour, though as drastic remedies for overweening conceit, boasting, or supposed cunning, they are not without occasional utility; but there should be no great intellectual disparity between the joker and his victim. To concoct a deliberate plot to befool such a numskull as Poinsinet, seems very like taking an elephant gun to kill a kitten.

It might be expected that the writings of one who was little better than an idiot would not possess any literary merit, but his works seem to have been appreciated fairly well. Sophie Arnould, who hated him, or at all events heartily despised him, declared that he stole all his verses. On one of the many occasions when he was reading his latest productions, a dog outside began to bark furiously.

"That is a good house-dog," said Sophie drily, "he has been taught to bark at a thief."

Probably he never stole anything more than

verses, though Mlle Duprat accused him of stealing her gold watch. He was acquitted of the charge, but was turned out of the "Academy" of Dijon, of which he was a member, all the same, and could not get re-instated. Perhaps he was too stupid even for a provincial assembly of *literati* and they were glad of the excuse to get rid of him.

On the 12th of September, 1764, died old Rameau, the greatest French musician of his time. Sophie Arnould made a very obvious and poor pun on his name when she heard of his death,* but it is doubtful if the compliment was sincere, for they had diametrically opposite ideas regarding opera. As her *forte* was feeling and expression she liked to take her airs at whatever time she thought best, and expected the orchestra to be subservient to her wishes. Rameau, on the contrary, cared little for either the singers or the words they had to utter, and relied on orchestral effects. He was accustomed to say that he could put the *Gazette de Hollande* to music, and it is recorded of him that at a rehearsal of one of his operas, he shook a basso who had a very loud voice, and said, pettishly, "Don't make so much noise. How are the people to hear my music?"

A few days later there died some very much less celebrated, and much younger musician, whose very name has escaped record, but whose death was made

* "Nos lauriers ont perdu leur plus beau Rameau."

the subject of a punning epitaph which is ascribed
to Sophie Arnould, though it is not in her style.
Indeed it is not altogether unlikely the man never
had any real existence, but was invented for the
purpose of the epigram.   The story runs that this
unknown musician was in love with a very pretty,
but very dissipated young actress, or dancer, of the
name of La Miré   His inordinate affection for this
young woman was supposed to have caused his
death, and Sophie Arnould, or someone else, suggested
that there should be cut on his grave-stone,

la mi ré la mi la

—which can also be read as

La Miré l'a mis là.

CHAPTER V.

OF the private life of Sophie Arnould during the next three years we know little or nothing. The Comte de Lauraguais was still her lover *en titre*, as is proved by the fact that he acknowledged himself the father of the child to whom Sophie gave birth in 1767, but it may reasonably be doubted whether each was all in all to the other during three years. Sophie would, we suspect, prove faithless occasionally, and the Comte would sometimes sigh for a mistress who was less witty, and not so high-spirited, and who would put up with his eccentricities, which Sophie had proved that she was certainly not willing to do. She would never have consented to be shut up in a green-house, and fed entirely upon hot-house fruit which was an experiment he had tried on one of his mistresses, who did at last complain of the régime, and was reproached with not being satisfied when she had all the luxuries

of life whilst so many people could not procure even
the necessaries.

Nor does Sophie appear to have done a distressing
amount of operatic work during the year 1765 at
least   On March 22nd she reappeared on the stage
after an absence of nearly twelve months, in Rameau's
ever-successful opera of *Castor et Pollux*, in which
she played the part of Zelaire,—one of her greatest
stage-triumphs.   Garrick was then in Paris, and was
making a rather long stay, for Collé mentions* that
he dined with him on January 5th.   The dinner was
not a success, for Collé had invited several guests
to hear the great actor recite, and Davy was naturally
huffed, refused to be trotted out, and showed so
much temper that Collé said it was the dullest
dinner he had ever eaten; and called himself a fool
for having invited an actor so disobliging, and bored
himself with talking about England to *ces deux
animaux-là*,—Garrick and his wife.

Like all actors, Garrick went frequently to the
theatre whilst in Paris.   He is reported to have said
that Sophie Arnould was the greatest actress on the
French stage.   On being asked why he preferred
her to the great tragic actress, Mlle Clairon, he
replied that the latter was too "stagey."   He must
have formed his estimate of Sophie's talents from
seeing her in this opera

Mlle Clairon he doubtless saw in the *Siege of*

* *Journal et Mémoires*, vol. iii, p. 2.

Calais, a drama by du Belloi, of no great literary merit, but a prodigious success, as it appealed to those Chauvinist feelings which are inherent in every Frenchman's heart. But if it did not possess much interest, there were several dramatic incidents connected with it, which, as they afforded Sophie Arnould opportunities of making some of her little jokes, must be briefly mentioned.

An actor, named Dubois, who played a secondary part in the piece, had incurred a heavy bill for "medical attendance." The surgeon, being unable to get his money, brought an action at law. Dubois declared on oath that he had paid the bill; the plaintiff swore equally hard that he had never received the money, and conclusively proved that the actor had committed perjury. His fellow actors considered that he had dishonoured the profession in general, and the house of Molière in particular,—a decision much to the amusement of Collé, who, though a dramatic author, had a curious contempt for actors, and professed himself unable to see how actors could have any honour at all, "unless honour, like the nails, could grow again." Three of the principal members of the company,—Le Kain, Molé, and Brizard,—and the leading lady, Mlle Clairon, thereupon besought the permission of the "Gentlemen of the Chamber," who in those days had the control of dramatic performances, to turn Dubois out of the troupe, and this permission was duly given.

For a few nights the piece was played with another
actor in the part that Dubois had taken, when one
morning orders came from the Gentlemen of the
Chamber that Dubois was to be re-instated and
resume his part. As usual, there was a woman at
the bottom of the affair Dubois had a very pretty
daughter, and she prevailed upon the Duc de Fron-
sac, who was one of the "committee", to order her
father to be restored to his place. The Duc had
no difficulty in persuading some of the other Gentlemen, and the order was sent to the comedians.
The actors went and saw the Minister, but he declined
to interfere, so they took the matter into their own
hands When the time came for the curtain to go
up, Le Kain, Molé, and Brizard were not in the
house. Mlle Clairon was, but, when she learned
what step her comrades had taken, she ordered her
chair and went home.

The other actors had assembled, and one of their
number was sent on the stage to announce that a
stock-piece would be played, but the public had
come to see the *Siege of Calais* and nothing else
would satisfy them. Shouts of "Clairon to prison,"
were raised, there was almost a riot, and finally the
theatre was cleared by the soldiers, and all money
returned.

But in those days it was dangerous to assert
one's independence Sophie Arnould said, "it was
the first time she had ever heard of a mutiny on

the day of a siege." The mutiny was promptly punished by the four ringleaders being sent to prison. When the "exempt" came to arrest Mlle Clairon, and escort her to Fort l'Evêque, she assumed a "tragedy queen" attitude, and cried, "The King may do what he pleases with my person, or with my property, but my honour he cannot touch."

Sophie Arnould, when she heard of this speech, said. "Of course he can't. Where there are no effects the King cannot seize." In some accounts, this remark is ascribed to the "exempt," but is more likely to have been uttered by the actress,—if indeed it was ever said by either.

Mlle Clairon and the others were released twenty-four hours later, and the performances of the *Siege of Calais* were resumed, Dubois very wisely refraining from forcing his obnoxious presence on the company. The play was a prodigious success, though its high-flown sentiments were not invariably clothed in a language which was poetical, or even grammatical. The witty Duc d'Ayen having said at Court that he did not like the *Siege of Calais* was told by Louis XV that he was "not a true Frenchman."

"Sire," was the reply, "I wish all the verses in the play were as truly French as I am."

Perhaps the success of the *Siege of Calais* may have had a good deal to do with some of Sophie Arnould's many "indispositions," for she did not care about playing to bad houses. At the Italian

Opera at this time they were playing an operatic version of *Tom Jones*, the music by Philidor, and the libretto by Poinsinet. Sophie said that Poinsinet was not at all likely to raise the Siege of Calais, and as a matter of fact *Tom Jones* fell very flat at first, but as the popularity of the *Siege of Calais* waned, business at the Italians began to improve, and Philidor's opera scored a moderate success.

Early in May Sophie handed over her part in *Castor and Pollux* to Mlle Durance and did not reappear till June 1st when she sang in an opera by Rameau entitled *Les Dieux d'Egypte* During the next two months she sang in one or two other operas by the same composer, there being a great demand for Rameau's work now that he was dead. On October 10th she appeared before the King and Court at Fontainebleau, in the opera of *Thetis and Peleus*. This was an old opera by Colasse, the words by Fontenelle, and was originally produced in January 1686, but had been " revived " on several occasions since, notably in 1750 when Fontenelle witnessed the performance. This we should imagine was " a record," for it is not given to every dramatic author to see one of his pieces played nearly sixty-five years after its first production.

The opera played at Fontainebleau was a revised version of this old opera, with new music by an anonymous composer, who, it was an open secret, was no other than M. Laborde, the King's valet.

Sophie Arnould, who played *Thetis*, was the critic
of the *Mercure* asserts,—the chief attraction of the
piece, and endowed that "great creation" with all
the graces of her genius, but the Court did not
appreciate the Valet's music, though the King—who
was presumably not more bored than usual,—applauded
frequently, and declared it was a very fine work.
This enthusiasm was thought to be assumed, "out
of consideration for M. Laborde," and if so Louis
is hardly to be blamed, for it must be manifestly
inconvenient to be shaved by a valet whose opera
you have damned, though such an eventuality is not
likely to occur frequently.

Sophie also sang at Fontainebleau a week later,
in a new opera entitled *Sylvie*, and with such success
that the work was "underlined" for performance in
Paris, but for some reason or other—perhaps on
account of the frequent indispositions of Mlle
Arnould,—was not played at the Opera House till
eighteen months later. The following week (24th
October), she again appeared before the Court as
Palmire in a new opera of the same name, and on
November 2nd in a new "heroic ballet," called
Zénis et Almasie, also the work of the royal valet,
Laborde. *Palmire* was at once produced in Paris,
but Sophie, as usual, pleaded ill-health after only
three performances, and her part was given to an
"under-study," Mlle Beaumesnil, who made her *début*,
and, who, as she was "as pretty as a flower," had

a good voice which would still further improve in time, and was remarkably self-possessed, at once became a popular favourite, and was rather a thorn in the side of Sophie Arnould, who was by no means free from professional jealousy.

Perhaps Mlle Beaumesnil's success cured Sophie Arnould's indisposition, for she appears to have returned to the theatre and fulfilled all her engagements during the next three months, and created one or two parts in one-act opera ballets, such as *Eglée, or the Triumph of Flora*, and the *Fêtes of Hymen*. During one of the performances of this latter piece, an accident happened to Mlle Guimard, one of the leading ballet-dancers. A piece of scenery fell on her, and broke her arm. Sophie, who was not above saying a spiteful thing when occasion offered, remarked that, "It was a pity it was not her leg instead of her arm, for then she could have danced as well as ever." Guérin the surgeon of the King's Musketeers, chanced to be in the theatre when the accident occurred, and set the limb at once. In a month or less Mlle Guimard was dancing with her arm in a sling, and a few days later was able to discard the sling. We shall hear a good deal more about her in the course of this narrative.

From the 4th to the 14th February 1766, Mlle Arnould was again absent from the theatre and her parts were being played by Mlle Durance, and a fortnight later she had another holiday, but this

was a compulsory one, for all the theatres were closed
from the 1st to the 13th of March on account of the
deaths of the Dauphin, and the Duke of Parma—
perhaps not altogether to the dissatisfaction of the
managers, for theatrical business was not exception-
ally good. At the Italian Opera house it was,
indeed, very bad, several of the new pieces could
hardly be called successes though they managed to
hold the stage for a few nights, and one—*La Garde
Chasse et le Braconnier*—was so thoroughly and effectively damned on the first night that it was never
played again. "It is strange we hear no more of
the 'Poacher'," some one observed in the green-
room one night.

"Probably he has been sent to the galleys,"
replied Sophie.

"*Aline, Queen of Golconda*, a heroic ballet in three
acts, music by Monsigny, words by Sedaine," was
performed for the first time on 15th April. In plot
it was an eighteenth century "prettiness,"—an
idyll that bore traces of the patch-box and the
powder puff. Aline is a young shepherdess who,
whilst tending her flocks in one of the valleys of
Golconda, makes the acquaintance of a young
stranger; they mutually fall in love, swear undying
fidelity to each other, and then part. Aline, some-
how or other becomes Queen of Golconda, and the
young man comes to her Court as Ambassador
from a neighbouring kingdom. He has not forgotten

his early love, but being naturally unprepared for
such a very remarkable change of fortune, does not
recognise in the Queen the shepherdess of former
days He neglects his ambassadorial functions and
takes to haunting the valley, which is seemingly
conveniently near the royal palace, in the hopes of
meeting his lady-love. Of course Aline dons the
dress of the shepherdess, meets her lover, and he
quits the diplomatic service in order to become
Prince Consort of Golconda.

From a stage point of view the part of Aline
would be very effective in the hands of a clever
actress, and Sophie Arnould could be relied on to
make the most of her opportunities. " She endowed
Aline," says one critic, " with all the delicate graces
of sentiment, beauty, and talent," and was tender
and loving as the shepherdess and noble and
dignified as the Queen. That this was not the mere
gush of a critic who was too susceptible to Sophie's
charms, is conclusively proved by the fact that the
opera had 26 consecutive representations, which in
those days was considered a long run

A little later, (June 17th), Sophie achieved another
success in one of those extraordinary pieces appro-
priately called Fragments, and which consisted of
three small one act operettas devoid of any con-
necting plot, and often indeed by different composers
and authors In one of these operetta-ballets entitled
Zelindor, Sophie Arnould played the leading part

(*Zurphé*), and, says a critic, the part could not have been acted with more taste, delicacy, art, and sentiment. She was rapturously applauded, but after a few performances, real or pretended indisposition prevented her from singing. Mlle Rosalie, or Rosalie Levasseur,[*] who was eventually to become the rival and enemy of Sophie Arnould, and deprive her of the chance of creating some of the heroines in Gluck's operas, made her first appearance in one of these "Fragments."

After a few of these temporary absences Sophie Arnould, on August 22nd, entirely gave up the part of *Zurphé* which on that evening was first played by Mlle Beauvais, who was so nervous that "timidity entirely absorbed all her faculties," which caused the absence of Mlle Arnould to be more than ever regretted.

In November, Sophie played for a few nights and sang three times in the Opera of *Sylvie*, a part she had created at Fontainebleau a year previously, but her performances lacked force and vigour, and even the critic of the *Mercure* was forced to find excuses for her, and plead that during the convalescence following a nervous malady, the actress was not in a fit state to do justice to her parts.

The prolonged rest which she then took (November

---

[*] She was at first known only as "Mlle Rosalie," but as that name was afterwards used for one of the characters in a comedy called *Les Courtisanes*, played at the Comédie Française, she resumed her surname, and was henceforth called "Mlle Levasseur." Sophie said, that, "she would have done better to change her face than change her name."

1766, to August 1767) is accounted for by the fact
that her fourth child, and only daughter, Alexandrine
Sophie, was born March 7th, 1767. Sophie usually
took a long holiday on these occasions and did not
act for several months both before and after her
confinement. She differed in this respect from one
of her fellow-actresses, Mlle Allard, whose engagement was at last cancelled by the managers on the
ground that her deplorable habit of producing two
children every eighteen months caused her to be
constantly in a condition which was destructive of
all stage effect. The almost chronic ungracefulness
of her figure also estranged the affections of her
lovers, and caused Sophie Arnould to say of her
that "she was like certain nations, always extending
her borders but never retaining her conquests."

On August 18th, 1767, Mlle Arnould's name was
again in the bills, and she appeared as *Pomona* in
a new opera ballet called *La Terre*. The *Mercure*,
as was usual, found in her all the old graces of
voice and face, combined with touching and natural
expression, and a less partial critic admits that no
performance could be more pleasing or better acted.
But the old nervous disease returned, and in less
than a month (September 15th) we find Mlle
Rosalie taking her place. This quickly brought
Sophie back in time to create a new part in a
"fragment" called *Amphion*, but she did not stay
long, for during the performance of 16th November,

her foot was injured by the fall of a piece of scenery, and she had a valid excuse for retiring. Her part was given to Mlle Durancy a versatile lady who was equally at home in opera or tragedy, and was always flitting between the Comédie Française and the Opera house.

This unlucky accident put a stop to the rehearsals of *Ernelinde, Princess of Norway*, which Poinsinet and Philidor had written specially for Sophie Arnould. The name of Philidor is no doubt known to many Englishmen, but not in connection with music. His real name was François André Danican, but the family had for three or four generations assumed the name of Philidor. In the time of Louis XIII, there was in the King's private orchestra an Italian flautist of the name of Filidori, of whose performances the King was very fond. Filidori died, and a musician named Danican, who was considered an excellent flautist was selected to take his place. The first time he played before the King, Louis XIII was so delighted that he cried: "Why he is as good as my Filidori," and the musician was so pleased with the compliment that he from henceforth assumed the name of Philidor,—a Frenchified form of Filidori. For several generations the family continued to produce musicians of respectable, but not startling, merit. François André, when a boy of nine or ten years of age, was appointed one of the "pages" in the private band of Louis XV. The pages had to give out the music, turn over the leaves, and otherwise render themselves generally useful, and occasionally sing glees or part songs. The band played to the King whilst he dined, and the musicians were expected to be in readiness, in an ante-chamber, a very considerable time before they were wanted. To beguile the time, several of the musicians used to play chess together, and little Philidor, having nothing else to do, watched them, soon learned the moves, and began to take an absorbing interest in the contests.

One night it happened that one of the players was late from some cause, and his usual antagonist was lamenting bitterly that there was no one to play chess with him. Little Philidor, then barely ten years of age, asked if he might take the absent player's place.

"You!" said the old musician, scornfully, "What do you know about chess? However, you can try what you can do. It will pass five minutes, anyhow."

The game began, and at the end of half a dozen moves the old player found that his victory would not be so easy as he had anticipated. Half a dozen moves later he began to realize that he must attend to the defence of his own King; and when eighteen or twenty moves had been made on each side, the boy rose cautiously from his seat, made a move, cried, "Checkmate," and rushed away, holding his

arms over his head, to protect it from the chess-
men, which the old musician—indignant at finding
himself mated by a boy of ten—hurled after him.

As he grew up his passion for chess increased.
He composed plenty of operas, but his heart was
not in his work.   He wrote a book about the game,
and has given his name to one of the "openings"
in the King's Knight's Game.* He visited London,
and astonished the players of the day by playing
three games blindfold.   Whilst Camille Desmoulins
was inciting the populace, Philidor was sitting at
the Café de la Regence, barely two hundred yards
away, calmly playing chess.   When the Revolution
broke out he returned to England, lived a few years
on a small pension given him by the London Chess
Club, died August 31st, 1795, and was buried, it
is said, in the churchyard of St. James's Church,
Piccadilly.

On December 26th, Sophie Arnould, having
recovered from the effects of her accident, made
her first appearance in a "boy's part,"—as *Colin*
in *Le Devin de Village*.   She had previously tried
the girl's part with no great success, and therefore

---

* The opening known as Philidor's Defence $\left\{ 1 \dfrac{\text{P to K 4}}{\text{P to K 4}} \quad 2 \dfrac{\text{Kt to K B 3}}{\text{P to Q 3}} \right\}$
was invented by Ruy Lopez, but the French player devoted such study
to it that his name remains associated with it.   Philidor's Defence is rarely
used by modern players, being considered "unsound." It does give the
second player a somewhat cramped game, but, though now neglected, it
was very successfully employed by Morphy against such antagonists as Harr-
witz and Lowenthal.

determined to try the boy's. The *Mercure* was lavish in its praises, but it may be doubted whether the performance was quite as successful as that rather partial critic declared it to be. She seems only to have played *Colin* for a fortnight, never repeated the experiment, and was always extra sarcastic if any of her fellow actresses donned male attire, and achieved a hit. Mlle Allard, a pretty and clever young woman, whose very numerous "love affairs" had astonished, and almost shocked, even the nymphs of the Opera, was once boasting in the green-room of the success she had met with in a boy's part she was then playing.

"I am sure half the audience thought I was a man," she declared.

"Perhaps so, dear," said Sophie, maliciously, "but the other half *knew* you were not."

Another story, much to the same effect, is that Mlle Allard had a full length portrait of herself, "in the nude" painted by a leading artist of the day, and invited all the *artistes* of the Opera, and the loungers of the green-room, to see the picture. One of the gentlemen remarked that the artist did not seem to have been very fortunate with Mlle Allard's face.

"That is not of much consequence," said Sophie Arnould, "half Paris would recognise Mlle Allard if the head had been left out altogether."

Like all professional wits, however, Sophie would

just as soon make a joke at the expense of virtue as of vice, if the opportunity offered. One of the dancers at the Opera was a very pretty, and very modest young woman, of no great intellectual attainments. She seems to have had some good sense as well as good principles, for finding herself beset by temptations, she very wisely married a young man who could look after her, and prevent the young bloods, who were always to be found behind the scenes, from making improper proposals to her. Some one praised her conduct in Mlle Arnould's hearing.

"Yes," replied Sophie, "we often find great virtues in 'simples.'"

CHAPTER VI.

(1768—1769)

THE first "slash of the penknife" to the irregular union subsisting between Sophie Arnould, and the Comte de Lauraguais, had been the act of the former;—the second and more serious rupture was caused by the Comte's notorious fickleness. Sophie does not seem to have made any marked effort to return the affections of her wayward and crotchety lover, beyond, perhaps, making some sarcastic remark about any young woman who momentarily attracted his attention. It is more than likely that a change was heartily desired by both parties, and that Sophie was quite as anxious to find a new lover, as the Comte was to take a new mistress. But if such were not the case she was, at least, not unprepared for such an eventuality, for the Comte had already, early in 1767, shown an inclination to be off with the old love, by indulging in a love affair with a young ballet dancer of the Opera, named Mlle Robbi. The *liaison* only lasted a few days or weeks, but it served to show Sophie that her influence over her lover had waned, and that he would leave her for some younger and fairer rival.

Nor did she have to wait long. On 26th February 1768, a Mdlle Heinel made her first appearance on the Paris stage. She was a ballet dancer, and although not more than seventeen or eighteen had already achieved a reputation in Vienna. The writer in Bachaumont's Chronique (possibly Abbé Voisenon) says of her: "Mlle Heinel is afflicted with seventeen or eighteen years, two large expressive eyes, and two well-shaped legs, which support a very pretty figure and face. She has come from Vienna to make her *début* in *danse noble*, and displays a precision, sureness, *aplomb*, and dignified bearing comparable only to that of the great Vestris." The charm of her dancing lay in her slow and graceful movements. Horace Walpole, who saw her in London at a later date, says of her; "She can turn as slowly as the Zodiac—but she is not the Virgin."

These varied charms, added to an "almost colossal stature," completely captivated the susceptible Lauraguais, for within a month of her first appearance Bachaumont was able to announce that the Comte had quite forgotten Mlle Arnould, and had given the German girl a "wedding present" of 30,000 livres, together with an apartment exquisitely furnished,

and a handsome equipage, and to this liberality added
a gift of 20,000 livres to one of her brothers, to whom
she was much attached.   In return for these gifts,
the lady bestowed upon him—so the scandal-mongers
asserted—a very unpleasant skin-disease for which
sulphur is usually recommended.   On the whole he
was estimated to have spent 100,000 livres on the
young German dancer, though she had modestly
fixed her own price at 14,000 livres.

Sophie Arnould appears to have hardly acted at
all during the year 1768, but whether her absence
was caused by ill-health, or quarrels with the other
members of the Company, or due to her having
found a fresh lover, it is impossible to say.   Possibly each of these causes counted for something.
Le Gros, the principal tenor, had been so much
annoyed by some of Sophie's sharp sayings that
he refused to act with her, and as the Opera possessed plenty of soprani and very few good tenors,
the Directors, after one or two vain attempts to
effect a reconciliation, produced *Dardanus* with
another *Iphise*.   Not until the very end of the year
(December 27th) did Mlle Arnould reappear, and
then she met with a reception which was almost a
triumph.

Such successes were rare in those days, for during
the years which intervened between the death of
Rameau and the advent of Gluck, French opera
was in a bad way, and no works of any merit were

produced. The audiences too, had tired of the woes of classical personages, and Fragments of interminable length, and Rebel, the manager of the Opera, wisely curtailed the operatic part of the programme and trusted to what one critic called the " noble but suggestive dancing of Mlles Guimard and Heinel, to restore the fallen fortunes of the theatre." As Sophie Arnould said, " the best way to support the Opera was to lengthen the ballets and shorten the skirts." The winter was very long and severe, and this also perhaps did not tend to make business any better at the Opera House. It should be mentioned that Mlle Guimard, who though notoriously unchaste was very charitable, gave away upwards of 8000 francs to the poor of the quarter in which she lived. Sophie Arnould imitated her, and also gave away large sums, and for this purpose visited the Hôtel Dieu. When she was passing through the lying-in ward, she turned to the nun who accompanied her, and said, " It is not here that you regret your vows of chastity."

At first Sophie absented herself from the theatre in order that she might not " grace the triumph" of Mlle Heinel, and perhaps for fear of the sneers she was sure to hear in the green-room, for, like all sarcastic people, she felt deeply any sarcasms which were levelled at her. She did not, as far as we know—for records of her private life are very difficult to find—take a new lover immediately, but

lived a few miles out of Paris, or at least made frequent
excursions into the country. It was on one of these
occasions that she found the poet who is usually called
"Gentil Bernard"+ lying under a tree, and asked him
what he was doing. "I was talking to myself," replied the poet. "Take care!" said Sophie, "for I
fear you are talking to a flatterer." Another time she
met a doctor with whom she acquainted. He was
crossing the wood on his way to visit a patient, and
being an ardent sportsman, carried a gun, in case
he came across any game on his road. Sophie
asked him where he was going, and he replied that
he was bound for a neighbouring village to see a
sick man. The actress glanced at the gun, and
said quietly, "And are you afraid of missing him?"
In these, as in many other of Sophie's sayings, it
is evident that she understood brevity was the soul
of wit, for the witticism was conveyed in the fewest
possible number of words.

Mlle Heinel had nothing but her physical attractions—her eighteen years, and her stately figure—
and her volatile, eccentric lover soon tired of her.
In less than a year the intrigue had come to an end,
and we find Sophie who had still preserved friendly
relations with her old admirer, and had promised
to let him know all that went on in Paris—perhaps

His real name was Pierre Joseph, but the nickname of "Gentil" bestowed upon him by Voltaire (though the Prince de Ligne says it was most
inappropriate) has clung to him so effectually that it has come to be regarded
his proper name.

he was undergoing one of his many short terms of
exile or imprisonment—making real or pretended
guesses concerning Mlle Heinel's latest protector
It may be, that reading between the lines, we can
detect some feminine spite, and the trace of a hankering after her old lover.

Thursday, March 2, 1769

You must have totally forgotten me, dear Comte,
for I have received no news of you since your
departure, and yet I have already sent you one of
poor Sophie's scrawls, as you asked me before you
left. I hoped that it would, at least, be worth a
short answer, in which you would give me news
of your health. That would interest me; as for
other news it is beyond me, for frankly speaking I
am a bad politician, and do not understand business
of any kind. As to the sort of news for which you ask,
it has been very scarce in Paris. Mlle Heinel is the
only one of all our ladies who has been at all talked
about for some time past. She has made choice
of a new lover—but the affair has been kept so
secret that I do not know the name of the lover—
three or four have been named, but there is no
positive knowledge as to who the Amphitryon really
is. Some say the Prince de Conty, others the Duc
de Condé, others M. d'Estinville, others Randon
d'Amecourt, in fact there is such a chaotic mass
of lovers that no one can discover the truth Folks

begin, however, to say that it is neither of
the two last named, and we are still in suspense
as to which of the first two is the lucky man.   For
my own part I would bet on Conty—who, I believe,
has done the thing in the most magnificent style,
for he has, it is said, given a hundred thousand
francs, cash down, a house of a hundred and thirty
five in the Rue de Richelieu, looking on the Palais
Royal, bought for her, furniture to match, and a
carriage and splendid horses.   The fool (whoever he
is) pays for everybody, I should imagine, and if it
is the Prince de Conty, that does not prevent him
from having his box open to all his concubines,
amongst whom I have sometimes the honour to be
numbered.   I can assure you that his manner of
kissing has not altered; some receive a salute on
the forehead, others on the eyes, others on the neck:
as for me I always have it on the tip of the chin,
and shall keep to that spot for a long time I expect,
—you would not advise me I suppose to come
down lower.   But a truce to joking which I only
permit myself with you, because I am sure that they
will be buried along with my stupidities, and that
you will preserve the strictest secrecy about both

If I did not fear to profane my heroines I should
make some mention of those of the Français, and
inform you that Mme. Vestris [*] has somewhat fallen

This Mme. Vestris was a Mlle Dugazon, who had married a brother
Gaetano Vestris, "the god of dancing." She is described by Grimm as

in public estimation; that Mlle Dubois reappeared last Sunday in *Inès de Castro* and had a great success, was unanimously praised, and applauded enough to bring down the ceiling; that the comedians have reproduced the *Siege of Calais* which again met with success. There is some talk of a piece called the *Deserter* which is to be produced on Monday next at the Italian Comedy. Mlle de C., the well-known actress of this theatre has married little Tual, but I feel that all this will not interest you so much as the doings of our sublime Academy: so consider that I have not told you anything.

Receive at least favourably the assurances of lifelong respect and esteem of your very affectionate

SOPHIE.

I send you herewith some verses made about Mlle Heinel. They are not very wonderful, treat them as the children of a foolish woman who is much attached to you. In any case you will not find the rhymes exact, but I give up that business, for I am not good at it, and out of all this folly I claim nothing but the choice of the tunes and the subject. It must be confessed that Sophie is an envious gazetteer—I own it and thereupon finish as well as my paper for— *

"not a consummate actress but an excellent *débutante*, with beauty, noble bearing, fine arms, and the most beautiful eyes in the world "

* An autograph letter in the collection of M A J Doucet quoted by E and J de Goncourt, *Sophie Arnould* pp 63 *et seq*

From this letter it would seem that the Comte had broken off with Mlle Heinel, and there appears to be some ground for the suspicion that Sophie still cared for her eccentric lover, and in spite of all his failings would have liked to have seen him once more at her feet. There is a good deal of feminine tact in the way in which she tries to excite his jealousy by mentioning the Prince de Conti. That Prince however, could hardly inspire jealousy in others, or feel it to any degree himself, for he is reported to have kept 60 "regular" mistresses, without counting the "minor," the "occasional" and the "imperceptibles,"—which, even in the Eighteenth Century was probably a "record" in that line so far as Europe was concerned.

It has been asserted that Sophie Arnould had a son by this "general lover," but there does not appear to be any foundation for the report except a wildly imaginative legend which is so obviously a *canard* that it is not worth consideration. The story is to the effect that some masons who were pulling down an old house, some thirty or forty years ago, discovered in the wall a small iron box which was strongly made and securely locked. Imagining that it contained money or jewellery, they, with considerable difficulty, broke it open, but found inside only a few old letters. In their disappointment they tore up these letters. The proprietor of the house, having been informed of the incident, came and gathered up the fragments as well as he could, and put them together, and found the document to be a letter of Sophie Arnould, in which mention was made of a son then at the Polytechnique, and who from the date could not have been one of the two surviving sons of the Comte de Lauraguais.

No allusion to such a son exists in any letter of Sophie's now extant, nor can any reference to him or record of him be discovered, so we may fairly conclude that he never existed. Sophie indeed, in her Memoirs, says that the Prince did think of devoting himself to her, but that he required that she should be "all his own, without any distraction or reserve." If he exacted a promise of that kind from all his manifold mistresses, he must either have been a great fool or a "new humourist." She declares that she refused his offer, because she "had no taste for exaggerated grandeur," but it is more likely that she did not care for the sixtieth part of a protector. The Prince, she says, always proved himself a good friend to her, gave her handsome presents, applauded her performances, and retailed her witticisms. In short, it would not be unnatural, or even uncharitable, to imagine that the name of the charming and witty actress was inscribed on the list of the Prince's "imperceptible" mistresses.

Mlle Heinel did not long excite the curiosity of her companions of the theatre as to her lovers, but assumed an outward semblance of respectability

7

at least, by marrying Gaetano Vestris. They had
quarrelled at first, and he had called her "*une calin*,"
nor, perhaps, did she find much consolation for her
wounded feelings in Sophie's sarcastic assurance,
"that people had grown so rude in these days that
they called things by their right names." She found
a powerful champion though, in the public, and
old Vestris was compelled, a night or two later, to
go down on his knees in the middle of the stage,
and apologize. It must have been a heavy blow to
his self-conceit, which was enormous, and about which
many amusing tales are told. Perhaps he was
ultimately drawn towards the young lady by hearing
her called "a Vestris in petticoats" which was given
her on account of her height. Both parties to the
quarrel presumably thought that if there was no
great love in the beginning yet heaven might decrease
it upon better acquaintance when they were married
and had more occasion to know one another, * and
a year or so later, Mdlle Heinel became Mme.
Vestris. Her amours are said to have been quite
as numerous, though less public, after her marriage.
Grimm gives a description, which is more graphic
than edifying, of the home life of the younger
Vestrises, and there is no reason to imagine that

Merry Wives of Windsor Act 1 sc 1 The source of the quotation
is given solely for the benefit of the reviewer of a certain literary journal,
who, lulled into a deceptive security by the absence of inverted commas,
lately cited a line from *Antony and Cleopatra* as a terrible example of
poor wit, indeed "

the morality of the family was sensibly augmented by the latest addition to its members.

Sophie Arnould cared very little for applause, and there is reason to think that she did not invariably exert her full powers on the few occasions when she did sing. Her beauty, dramatic force, and reputation for wit, made her as popular before the curtain as she was unpopular behind it. The difficulties of an *impressario* were less than they are in the present day, as a capricious *prima donna* could be sent to prison if she turned sulky, but it was obviously difficult, if not impossible, to know whether an artiste was doing his or her best. The suspicions of the managers must have been aroused in the many cases in which Sophie had pleaded indisposition on the second or third representation of a new opera, after singing splendidly at the first performance, and these suspicions were considerably strengthened by an incident which happened early this year (1769).

On February 5th she performed in *Erosine*, one of her old parts, and "played rather than sung it, her organ having absolutely refused to serve her." A fortnight later *Dardanus* was revived, and though it was one of her greatest parts, she either could not or would not sing, and the opera became "almost a burlesque."

But the second performance was very different. Thinking, possibly, that anyone was good enough to sing with a voiceless *prima donna*, the managers entrusted the part of *Dardanus* to a new singer named Muguet, who had neither "voice, figure, nor expression." His efforts met at first with derisive laughter, which turned into hisses, and yells. At this juncture a change came over Sophie. Her voice became clearer and louder than her admirers had ever known it, and her acting more impassioned. Badly seconded as she was, she succeeded in saving the opera from becoming an utter failure, and even converted it into almost a success. She afterwards told a friend that she could have done better still if Le Gros had been acting with her, as he was the only tenor who made her put out her full strength

Whatever may have been the cause, it is certain that the relations of Sophie with the management were far from friendly, and she talked of definitely retiring from the stage. The news caused considerable excitement, and several noblemen of the Court interested themselves on Sophie's behalf, and persuaded the managers to "pardon the vagaries of this amiable actress," and even induced Sophie—which must have been a more difficult task—"to make some concessions to the first-named " A reconciliation was effected, but Sophie stipulated that she should not be called on to perform before St. Martin's day (11th November) when the new Opera house was to be ready, when she promised to sing on the opening night in *Castor and Pollux*.

Perhaps she tired of inactivity, or found that there was no chance of the new theatre being ready by

the time named, for on 4th October she reappeared
in an "act" entitled *Psyché*, and added a fresh grace
to the piece by her inimitable acting. As she was
a great favourite with the public, and had not acted
for several months, and was never expected to sing
again in the Salle des Machines, she was received
with "indescribable transports." Her voice was
declared to be "more sustained and not less seduc-
tive" than ever, and her attitudes, which were "always
beautiful and full of interest" moved the souls of the
spectators and strongly excited them. Perhaps some
explanation of this exceedingly laudatory criticism
may be found in the fact that the words of the
operetta were by Abbé Voisenon, who collaborated
with Bachaumont in the production of the Mémoires
Secrets from which this extract is taken

A few days later, the same critic had a second short
but eulogistic notice on Sophie, who, it was stated,
had come from Fontainebleau in order to sing at
the Opera, and was going to return to Fontainebleau
directly after the performance. On the occasion of
her return visit to Court her sarcastic tongue brought
her into trouble. The King had but a few months
before been captivated by the charms of Madame
du Barry, and the last of the great "Queens of the
left hand" was at that time in the plenitude of her
power. Sophie Arnould had doubtless often seen
the royal mistress at the Opera when she was only
Mlle Lange, "the milch cow of Comte Jean du

Barry," and that astute blackleg used her as a lure for rich pigeons he wanted to pluck.

Sophie had very little respect for anyone, and looked upon the du Barry as being only "the luckiest kept-woman in France." In what manner she showed contempt for the royal favourite is not very clear, but she did display such "unexampled audacity" and such "essential want of respect" towards Madame du Barry, that the King ordered her to be imprisoned in the "Hospital" for six months.

The exact nature of her offence is not stated, but it is not unlikely that she owed her sentence to one of the many strange freaks of her late lover the Comte de Lauraguais. That eccentric personage had taken lodgings in the town of Fontainebleau for a young woman whom he had brought from Paris, and whom he had named, for the nonce, the Comtesse du Tonneau. The joke—as we have said elsewhere [1] was rather of the "Cyclopean order," but bad as it was, the King possibly thought that he had not invented it himself, and as he was known to be still in good terms with Sophie Arnould, though she was no longer his mistress, she had devised this cumbrous practical joke for him The supposition was partly borne out by the fact that Sophie had on this, or a previous occasion, made a very indifferent pun on the Favourite's name by saying that,

[1] _Life and times of Mme du Barry_, by R. B. Douglas, London, 1896

" When the barrel (*baril*) began to roll, the Chancellor would have his legs broken "

It could scarcely have been this mild joke which brought down the wrath of the King on the actress, for scores of more spiteful things were said about du Barry every day by the hired scribes of the Duc de Choiseul, besides which it was rather against the Chancellor" (de Maupeou) than the Mistress, that the remark was levelled, and he was no great favourite with the King, and was, moreover, perfectly capable of dealing with his own enemies.

In any case, the question is not of much importance, for Sophie never went to the Hospital or any other place of detention, or at most stopped there but a fear hours. Madame du Barry was very kind-hearted, and readily forgave all offences against her She appears to have taken a vow that no one should ever suffer for her sake, and, on hearing of the sentence on the popular *prima donna*, at once went to the King and implored him to forgive Sophie. She had some difficulty in gaining her point, but Louis could not withstand her pleading, and Sophie's pardon was signed. The Comte de Lauraguais had also been ordered to the Bastille, and the du Barry also interceded on his behalf, and succeeded in getting his sentence reduced to one of exile He was rather used to that, as he had been exiled on at least three previous occasions, and had always managed to obtain pardon after a few months' stay in England or elsewhere.

To the actors and actresses at the Opera the news of Sophie's disgrace was particularly pleasant. There was not one of them who had not often suffered from her sarcastic wit, and a retort which was within the capabilities of even the least witty was now afforded. With "marvellous charity" says Bachaumont or his "contributor," they took care to let fall the word "Hospital" whenever Sophie came within ear-shot, which no doubt "greatly humiliated that superb Queen of Opera." Their elation was possibly increased by the fact that Sophie had been punished for insulting or offending an "improper female." There was hardly one virtuous woman in the Opera, but they all assumed an outward appearance of decorum, and made the most of such shreds of reputation as they enjoyed, whereas Sophie Arnould always displayed a reckless cynical effrontery respecting morals, and shocked some of her equally frail sisters by her plain-speaking. It is recorded that a grand supper was once given to several singers and dancers of the Opera. The ladies were all magnificently dressed, and their fair necks and shoulders sparkled with jewels. The table was laden with the choicest wines and most delicate viands; the gentlemen were attentive and polite, and the conversation was what our forefathers used to term "elegant." Sophie was ill-tempered, and more than usually caustic, and horrified the lady guests by exclaiming in the midst of the banquet, "Anyone would think that we were all Princesses, or great ladies at the very least, whereas we are nothing better than a pack of—" The scene that followed was indescribable says the chronicler. Several of the ladies screamed; one developed symptoms of incipient hysteria, and even the calmest declared that they would not continue to sit at table with a person who made use of such disgusting language.

The expression which so much offended the sensitive ears of the frail actresses was one which Sophie often employed, and its use did not tend to make her any the more beloved. The Duc de Praslin once asked after a *fille de l' Opéra* with whom he had been acquainted, but whose name he had forgotten. He described her to Sophie as well as he was able, and concluded by saying that though he could not remember all the name, he knew it ended in "ain."

"Ah, monsieur le Duc," replied Sophie, "you must give a more exact description than that, or you will never find her. We all have a name that ends in 'ain."

At Fontainebleau a representation of *Dardanus* had been given before the Court, with the best "cast" obtainable. New and handsome costumes had been specially made for the occasion, and as the actresses were anxious to show their new dresses

to a Paris audience, His Majesty was asked to
graciously allow his subjects to witness a performance similar to that through which the King had
sedulously slept. Favours which cost nothing were
easily granted by Louis XV, and the performance
was duly given. Sophie Arnould exerted herself to
the utmost to gain the applause of the public, close
the mouths of her enemies, and obliterate the memory
of her recent adventure."

She may have succeeded, so far as the public
was concerned, but her fellow-actors and actresses
still continued to make allusions to the " Hospital,"
and Sophie temporarily retired from the stage for
more than two years How she spent that long
interval we cannot tell In all likelihood she began
that astonishing series of " transient amours " which
have made her name notorious even in the annals
of the French Stage; but if so we should expect
to find mention, and even frequent mention, of her
in the scandal-loving Bachaumont. But for some
twenty months (November 30th, 1769, to August 13th,
1771) her name is entirely absent from his pages,
and, when it does occur at last, it is to state that
the " Demoiselle Arnoux, so celebrated for her talents,
and who had laughed at so many people," will now
be a laughing stock herself, for she is going to be
married to a young fortune-hunter, whose only merit
was that he had the skill to captivate an actress
with a large fortune.

This report was utterly false, for Sophie Arnould was never married or—so far as we know—on the point of getting married, to any one, and it seems evident that the writer of the paragraph knew absolutely nothing about her private life.

Another difficulty which arises, is to account for her being able to take such a long rest without incurring the wrath of the managers, and getting locked up in Fort l'Evêque, but it must be remembered that MM. Rebel and Trial had been anxious to cancel her engagement, and had only been prevented from doing so by the intervention of some gentlemen of the Court. Besides which, they had themselves been thinking of retiring from the management of the Opera, the City of Paris having the intention of making it a municipal theatre.

At any rate no one tried to interfere with Sophie Arnould's liberty. The use she made of her freedom was to visit continually all the theatres of Paris. She might have been at the Théâtre Français when one of the actors came forward at the end of *Le Père de Famille*—a very successful, but now quite forgotten drama—to announce that on the following evening *Hamlet*, "with the fifth act entirely rewritten," would be given, and the pit rose like one man and yelled. "Not *Hamlet*—the *Père de Famille*!"

She certainly went to Lemierre's drama on *William Tell* in the winter of 1769. The legend was not much to the taste of French audiences, though doubt-

less it would have been twenty years later, and after
a few nights was played to half empty houses. The
author, to fill the house, distributed "paper" freely
amongst the Swiss to be found in Paris, who formed
enthusiastic but not profitable audiences. Sophie
Arnould who saw how the audience was composed,
remarked, "The proverb says, *Point d'argent, point
de Suisse;* but here there are plenty of Swiss and
no money."

Lemierre had often been the subject of her wit.
He told her once that d'Alembert had said, apropos
of Lemierre's *Hypermnestra*, that the author had "made
a step" in tragedy. "True!" replied Sophie, "but
is it forwards or backwards?"

It was on one of these visits to the theatre during
this winter that she saw the Abbé Terray, the
very unpopular Controller General of Finances. The
weather was bitterly cold—the winter was an extremely severe one,—and the Abbé had his hands
hidden in a large muff. "What need has he of a
muff?" she asked sarcastically. "Are not his hands
always in our pockets?"

No doubt she frequented the society of the leading
demi-mondaines, and was frequently at the magnificent
hotel which had recently been constructed for that
"skeleton of the Graces," Mlle Guimard. This
splendid edifice was in the Chaussée d'Antin, and
was called the "Temple of Terpsichore." It had
cost such an immense sum that, rich as Mlle

Guimard was known to be, it was doubtful whether
she would be able to discharge all her obligations,
and someone inquired, in Sophie's hearing, whether
it was likely that the *danseuse* would " honour all
her debts." " Of course, she will," replied Sophie.
" Guimard is the soul of honour, and will some
day die in a bed of honour."

She was also to be met at the Sunday dinners
known as " the Dominical," held at the house of
Louis, a celebrated surgeon, the guests being all
members of a harmonic Society.   One of the rules
of this Society was that no woman should be
admitted, but an exception was made in favour of
Sophie, and she was permitted to hear Crebillon fils,
Barré, Vadé, and Chaussepierre, sing songs of their
own composition.   Most of these productions were,
it may be guessed, " quite unfit for publication,"
and though the company was " good," in the social
sense, it may be doubted whether any respectable
woman would have cared for the privilege which
Sophie enjoyed.   But judging from some of her
witticisms, which it has been found quite impossible
to reproduce in these pages, it is pretty certain that
she was the least-likely person in the company to
have blushed if a more than usually broad joke was
blurted out, or an especially risky song was rattled
off.   When an " atrabilious moralist " inveighed in
the green-room against the depravity of the Stage,
and instanced the number of " improper females "

he saw there assembled, Sophie checked him by
remarking "Let the poor girls enjoy the loss of
their reputation." She consistently acted up to this
maxim, and perhaps never so much enjoyed the loss
of her own reputation as when she was sitting at
the table of the eminent surgeon.

CHAPTER VII.

OWING to the severe weather, the new Opera House was not ready at the date announced, and did not open till January 24th, 1770. The construction of the new theatre was adversely criticized. The boxes and pit were not well arranged and the gallery was so far from the stage that it "seemed to be in another world" Sophie Arnould said to Soufflot, the architect, "Ah, monsieur, what will become of us? We shall have to shout like all the devils in order to be heard in Paradise." The stage, however, was large and high—36 feet wide, by 32 feet high,—with plenty of conveniences for scenery and machinery.

Sophie—perhaps not wishing to "shout like all the devils"—did not sing at all during the year, except at one of the three "benefit nights" of the Company in March. If her health was bad, as she pretended, she hardly went the right way to work

to improve it. She had found a new "protector,"
in the person of "Charles Alexandre Marc Marcellin
d'Alsace et d'Hénin-Liétard, Prince d'Hénin et du
Saint Empire, Colonel of the French Grenadiers."
He was proud and priggish, but at least never flew
into violent passions, smashed the furniture, or as-
saulted Sophie. He kept a mistress, because in those
days it was considered "bad form" not to do so,
and to pose as the protector of a celebrated actress
was something almost akin to a virtue.

Jealousy was not, apparently, one of his failings,
and Sophie was permitted to do very much as she
liked, and she took full advantage of the permission.
She kept open house, and her table has not been
inaptly described by M. de Goncourt as "an altar
of free life and free love." Foreign ambassadors
covered her with diamonds, Serene Highnesses threw
themselves at her feet, Dukes and Peers sent her
carriages, and Princes of the Blood deigned to have
children by her." * There were few women, even
in those times when morality was at its lowest ebb,
who could vie with her in depravity, or who were so
recklessly and cynically indifferent to such poor shreds
of reputation as they still had. Once a young Gascon
gentleman was looking over the apartments and noticed
what a splendid "dome" there was over Sophie's bed.

* According to the *Chronique galante* she had a daughter by the Prince
de Condé, and this daughter eventually married the Comte de R.—There
is no evidence to confirm the story.

" Yes," replied the witty actress ; " and let me inform
you that it is not the dome of the Invalides either."

In the May of this year the Dauphin, afterwards
Louis XVI, was married to Marie Antoinette, and
of course there were great festivities both in the
Court and City. Perhaps Sophie acted at Versailles.
M. de Goncourt quotes a letter which was written
by the Comtesse du Barry to the actress telling the
fair Sophie to " surpass herself" as she had to act
" before the daughter of Emperors," but he hints
that he cannot quite understand the letter as Sophie
hardly acted at all that year. It is true that he has
post-dated the wedding by two years for the Dauphin
was married in 1770, not 1772 as he states, but
the difficulty is not removed by correcting the error,
for if Sophie Arnould acted very little in 1772, she
does not seem to have acted at all in 1770, or, if
she did, the event is not recorded either by Bachaumont or in the *Mercure de France*.

In December, 1770, the Duc de Choiseul was
disgraced and sent into exile—an act which is
usually ascribed to the influence of the du Barry,
but with which she really had nothing to do For
a short period after his fall, the Duc was a popular
idol-cum-martyr, and snuff-boxes were made, bearing
the Duc's portrait on one side, and that of Sully
on the other. Sophie was likely to be on the du
Barry side, for she owed some thanks to the fair
Comtesse for having interceded with the King on

her behalf, when the King wanted to send the prima
donna to prison for not showing respect to the royal
mistress. She said of these snuff-boxes that "they
had put the receipts and expenses together," which was
not a bad description of the extravagance of Choiseul
and the parsimony of the famous Minister of Henri IV.

In 1771, Sophie Arnould played in March in
Pyramus and Thisbe for one or two nights, and was
greatly applauded. As usual, her voice failed her,
and the critics regretted that "her health was not
strong enough to enable her to renew more frequently
those pleasures which her presence gives us." Mlle
Beaumesnil had to take her parts, but though she
had graceful attitudes and everything external that
an actress could need, the critics found her "devoid
of the soul necessary for the delicate shades of
expression, of which she was not capable."

Sophie came back to play on one of the "benefit"
nights, and drew an enormous audience to see
her perform *Psyché*, though the seats cost a louis
each. The receipts, says Bachaumont, exceeded six
thousand francs without counting the royal boxes,
but "six" is evidently a misprint for "dix," for
a line or two lower the writer states that on the
previous Saturday the receipts were only eight
thousand and some odd hundred francs.

She does not appear to have acted again, or at
all events not to have created any part, till she sang
in *Amadis de Gaule* at the end of November. The

opera was an old one of Lulli's, but Berton, one of
the Directors of the Opera, had rewritten the music
and brought it "up to date." Berton was not
Lulli by a long way, and though the tearful part
of *Oriana* was admirably played by Sophie Arnould
"who gave full force to the sublime apostrophe"—
one of the few things in the opera which Berton
had fortunately left alone—"the boldness of the experiment was not rewarded by success." * It seems,
however, to have been played several times, and,—
which is more remarkable still—Sophie continued
to sing in it, for in January 1772 the *Mercure* records that "Mlle Arnould, in spite of her weak
health, proves in the *rôle* of *Oriana*, how real talent
and resources will please."

In fact, on the few occasions on which she did
appear, Sophie gave evidence of that remarkable
talent which, a couple of years later, was to culmi-
nate in the personations of the heroines of Gluck's
operas, and to make her famous as a great tragic
actress, and the first exponent of modern opera.
Another instance of her great tragic power was
given in *Castor and Pollux* played in February.
The critic of the *Mercure*—who was, however, always
favourably disposed towards Sophie—wrote that
"she was not a character of the piece, but *Thélaire*
herself, and all the feelings she depicted passed involuntarily into the souls of the spectators."

* FÉTIS: *Dictionnaire des Musiciens* Art. *Amadis*.

This adulation made her conceited, and though she professed to be indifferent to applause and criticism, she could not help feeling that she was the pet of the public, and gave herself airs in consequence.

On the night of March 24th she refused to act, and did not, as on so many previous occasions, plead indisposition, but plainly showed that her conduct was actuated by no other motive than "pure caprice", by coming down to the theatre and taking her seat in one of the boxes. The managers sent to ask her what she meant by appearing in the front of the house when she was "billed" to play a part that evening, and she impudently replied that she had come to take a lesson of Mlle Beaumesnil, who was her "understudy." The managers thereupon complained to the Duc de la Vrillière, who, in his official capacity as Chamberlain, had the control of the King's music, and requested him to send the recalcitrant actress to Fort l'Evêque. That distinguished nobleman did an extensive and lucrative business in *lettres de cachet*, and issued orders for the Bastille at a fixed price of 50 louis, and for the minor prisons at a reduced tariff. He no doubt felt that it would be establishing a bad precedent to send anyone to prison unless he was paid to put them there, and, as the directors had not complied with that formality, he contented himself with giving Sophie a severe reprimand.

This leniency did not satisfy some "ill-natured spectators," who resolved to go to the theatre on the following Tuesday, and "humiliate" this proud and impertinent actress. They duly went, but Sophie, who perhaps wished to atone for her misconduct, put forth all the seductions of her voice, her beauty, and her dramatic talent, and the conspirators "had not the courage" to utter a single cat-call. "Her playing made them forget their project," and those who came to hiss remained to applaud.

It was at about this date that she uttered one of her most celebrated and daring witticims, which is well-known to all French readers. A little operetta, the music by Monsigny, words by Sedaine was produced at the Italiens on 19th March. The subject was the celebrated story of Boccaccio which tells how a lover, having nothing else wherewith to regale his mistress, killed and served his favourite hawk. Upon the title of this little piece Sophie made a very obvious pun which the intelligent reader will have no difficully in guessing, or, if he cannot, he may consult Bachaumont under date of 22nd March 1772.

Puns, though not quite of so broad a nature, formed no inconsiderable portion of the witticisms of Sophie Arnould, and she was addicted to that exceedingly poor form of wit, punning on names. A dozen examples occur to mind, but to quote them would be to bore the reader without

enhancing her reputation as a wit. One of the best
was on the steward of the Prince de Gulméne, who
was suspected to have made "pretty pickings" out
of his master's estate.

He yearned after literary honours, composed verses,
and even wrote the libretto of an opera, which he
requested a friend to read to Sophie Arnould. She
listened to it, and then said, "I fancy the author
has cribbed a few lines here and there, but taken
on the whole I am of opinion that the work is
worthy of a Voltaire "(*vole terre*)." If the author
did not see the pun he doubtless felt flattered, but
if he did detect the play upon words his feelings
must have been the reverse of pleasant.

Jokes upon such names as Lemoine, Lecoq, Chardon,
etc., do not merit to be recorded, but a good instance of
the pun as a vehicle for satire was afforded by her
joke at the expense of three sisters who joined the
corps de ballet, and had assumed the names of Rose,
Hyacinthe, and Marguerite. "What a flower border!"
cried Sophie Arnould when they were introduced
to her, but the word she used (*plate-bande*) was
capable of a less complimentary signification.

Castor and Pollux was a great success, principally
owing to the acting of Sophie Arnould, and the
house was crowded at every performance. Grimm
relates a story of a fat old tradesman who had never
been seen at the Opera before, and who could not
procure a seat but was obliged to stand in a large

box, called the *coche*, with some thirty other spectators. He endured the inconvenience during the first
act, but when the second act began with the funeral
of *Castor*, he called out, "Well! I have paid my
money, and I am being stifled and crushed to death,
and all to see a funeral, which I could see, comfor-
tably and for nothing, any day in the week, at Saint-
Roch."

There was a dance of demons in this opera, and
on the first night, the dance not having been sufficiently rehearsed, the demons became hopelessly
"clubbed." News had reached Paris that same
afternoon that the Duc de Vauguyon, a very unpopular nobleman, had died at Versailles. Sophie
sarcastically remarked, "The devils are so upset by
the arrival of the Duc de Vauguyon amongst them
that they have lost their heads."

For the next few months we again lose sight of
Sophie On November 17th, a *débutante*, Mlle
Virginie made her first appearance. In spite of her
nervousness it was evident that she had a good
voice, which had been well trained, and she met
with a favourable reception. "Much was hoped from
her," says one of the critics, "for she is a pupil of
Sophie Arnould," and he dilates upon what an
advantage to the public it would be if the leading
singers would devote their time to forming apt pupils.
It is to be hoped that Mlle Virginie only took lessons in music, and not in morals, from her mistress

Sophie was not present to see her pupil's success. Mlle Fleury had recently given birth to an illegitimate child, and as the Prince de Nassau was, or had been, one of her numerous lovers, she fathered it on him, and had his name inserted in the parish register as the male parent. Sophie had promised to stand godmother to the infant, but guessing that the Prince was not likely to be greatly pleased about the matter, she had prudently started for Spa about a fortnight before Mlle Fleury expected to be confined. Powerful personages were not lightly to be offended in days when the hinges of prison doors were kept well greased. As a matter of fact the Prince was highly indignant, and wanted to have the page of the register which bore his name torn out and destroyed, but finding that was impossible, he stormed and raved, abused his mistress, and quarrelled with a nobleman who, like Sophie, had promised to stand sponsor to the child, but unlike her, had kept his word, though he had been represented by proxy. Quarrels, at that time, were usually settled with the sword, but the Prince, though he had the reputation of being a very good swordsman, did not seem at all inclined to go out on this occasion, which called forth the remark from Sophie that "people with a very great talent for anything, always required a deal of pressing before they would show off."

Whether Sophie went to Spa to get out of the

way, or whether she went to benefit her health, she was, at all events, back in Paris within a week of the christening, and was announced to sing at the Opera on the night of Tuesday, December 1st. At any rate the visit to Spa does not seem to have done her any permanent good, for when *Adele de Ponthieu*, an opera by La Borde, the musical valet of Louis XV, was produced, she was unable to appear, though her name was down in the bills, and the part was played by Mlle Beaumesnil. That actress often had to understudy Sophie's parts during the year. Mlle Arnould's name occurs a few times in the course of the season. She sang a few times in *Castor and Pollux*, but the critics complained that her performances lacked their old fire, and Beaumesnil, or Rosalie Levasseur, was often called upon to take her place.

Her wit, however, was unimpaired and her mode of life was as luxurious and dissipated as ever. She was then living in the Palais Royal, apparently close to where the Palais Royal Theatre now stands. In October 1773 a son was born to the Duc d'Orléans, and Sophie requested permission to give a display of fireworks in the garden at the back of her house. The letter in which she demands this permission is couched in a half-impudent, half-flattering strain. She begins by reminding him that the Opera had been of use to him in supplying him with no fewer than three of his mistresses, Mlle Rosalie, and Mlles Deschamps and Marquise, who both belonged to the chorus. At the birth of kings, gold, myrrh, and frankincense were offered, but gold was too common, myrrh had not a very agreeable odour, and so many fair hands would be offering incense that she would not mingle with them. But, as her apartment was at the end of the garden, she craved leave to let off a display of fireworks, but though the fireworks would go out, the fire of admiration in her heart would never, etc., etc.

In the Eighteenth Century compliments of this kind were not considered cloying, and the Demoiselle Arnould obtained the required permission, and the rockets and squibs were duly let off, and attracted an enormous number of the frail sisterhood who haunted the arcades of the Palais Royal. This—more perhaps than the fireworks "marvellously delighted the amateurs," and cheers were given for the Demoiselle Arnould.

In fact, Sophie made the occasion of the birth of the Duc de Valois an opportunity for getting a good advertisement, of which she stood in some need, for owing to her infrequent appearances, she stood in some danger of being forgotten--professionally. Personally, or privately, she ran no such risk She gave balls and banquets at which were to be found all the pretty actresses and fast women of Paris, and representatives of the Court, the Camp, and the

Grove She held quite a small court, to which
resorted noblemen and gentry from the " Conqueror
of Minorca," grizzled in the service of Vice, to the
Gascon squireen who had come to Paris to solicit
a place With them were soldiers like Dumouriez —
an able commander, but a man who was not to be
trusted in word or deed; and the tall but stupid
Chevalier de Tiercin, of whom Sophie said he was
like a "tall house,—the rooms at the top are always
the worst furnished." *

There were also wits and authors; Marmontel,
Crebillon fils—" the dullest of indecent writers"—
Abbé Voisenon, who was only dull when he wrote
verse, and only indecent when he wrote prose,—
Abbé Arnoud, who was shortly to take up the
cudgels for Gluck and the new school of music, and
Dorat—" cold and polished as marble" (so Sophie
said), but whose verses were certainly warm.

Dorat was a great admirer of Sophie, and
would sit moody and silent, and refuse to eat when
he saw the actress flirting with some rich or powerful lover. This affection was not well rewarded.
When his Fables were produced this year (1773)
they fell very flat, though some copies were bought
for the sake of the engravings, which were deemed
excellent. Sophie Arnould said, " le pauvre Dorat

* The remark was probably original with her, but Thomas Fuller had
written, a hundred and odd years before,—' Often the cockloft is empty in
those whom Nature hath built many stories high," and he had taken the
idea from Bacon (*Apothegm* No. 17)

se sauve par les planches." Another time when
some one complained, in the presence of the author,
of the high price of the book, Sophie chimed in
with : " Why only look at the paper, the engravings
and the vignettes! They alone are worth all the
money, and the verses are given away gratis."

CHAPTER VIII.

We have now come to the time when Sophie Arnould is to attain to the zenith of her professional fame. The school of French Opera, of which she had hitherto been an exponent, had few merits except its tunefulness, and if she had reached any height of dramatic expression in the rendering of the works of Rameau, Philidor, and Lulli, she had derived little or no support from the orchestra. With the advent of Gluck, a remarkable change came over French opera. It is not the place to estimate the genius of the great German composer, nor is there any need to discuss questions over which much good ink was spilled, but which time has settled unalterably. The grand and simple melodies of Gluck superseded the jingling pretti-

nesses of the earlier French and Italian schools, but
not without a struggle which was short and sharp,
and in which all the leading literary men of France
took part.

The most able pens—those of Marmontel, d'Alam-
bert, and La Harpe—were enlisted on the side of
Piccini, the Italian composer who was summoned in
hot haste to counteract the influence of the favourite
musician of Marie Antoinette, but their efforts to
bolster up their champion were ineffectual, and Gluck
remained the master of the field.   Probably the
Queen's predilections had little to do with the result—
the question was decided by the public ; but it is
not unlikely that the victory of Gluck was rendered
far more complete by the intensity and dramatic
force which Sophie Arnould was able to throw into
the characters of the heroines of the Master's works,
which, it should be recollected, he described as
not operas but " musical dramas."

That the genius of Gluck would eventually triumph
over the " traditions " of the old French opera, was
beyond a doubt, but he was fortunate in having
the assistance of Sophie Arnould.   Both composer
and artiste held opinions regarding their art which
were decidedly in advance of the time in which
they lived.

It is related of Sophie Arnould that, during the
last days of 1773, she was rehearsing in *Cephalis
et Procris*, an opera by Grétry, for a performance

which was to be given before the King and Court on December 30th. At one of the rehearsals she stopped the orchestra and addressing Francoeur, the conductor, said:

"What is the meaning of this, Monsieur? There is a rebellion in your orchestra"

"What do you mean by a rebellion, Mademoiselle? We are here to serve the King, and we serve him zealously."

"I also want to serve him, but your orchestra puts me out, and prevents me from singing"

"Nevertheless, Mademoiselle, we were keeping the time."

"The time? *Quelle bête est-ce cela?* Follow me, if you please, and learn that your accompaniment is nothing more than the servant of the actress who is reciting."

Whether Francœur gave in or not, history does not state, but most likely he did. Castel Blaize, a musical critic, and the author of several works concerning the Opera, is of opinion that it was this habit of not adhering strictly to time which caused Gluck to eventually deprive Sophie of her parts in his operas and give them to younger artistes, who would not sacrifice singing to acting.

"She had been accustomed to lengthen or shorten her notes according to her feelings, or the condition of her voice," says the critic just quoted, and therefore her dramatic talent "became superfluous" when she had to keep time like "a simple coryphée".

To make the theory plausible, the anecdote given above ought to have been dated some ten or twelve years earlier. During the fifteen years she had been on the stage she must either have been one of "men and women reciting a tragedy musically to intonations indicated by a musician,"* or there was a conductor who understood her, and complied with a custom which is now general. If she had only acquired this habit of singing without regard to the orchestra at a time when Gluck was actually in France—for he was not improbably present at this very performance of *Cephalis et Procris*—and only four months before she appeared in his first opera, she would have found it easier to revert to her old habits than lose her parts. But, as a matter of fact, she continued to sing in Gluck's operas for about four years, and, when she was at last superseded, there were at least two adequate, besides two inadequate, reasons for such a step.

The chief one was that her voice, which was never very strong, was quite unable to bear the strain which the dramatic situations even more than the music, put upon it. Another reason was that her disorderly life made her careless and negligent of her professional duties, and more over-bearing than ever Minor reasons might be found in the fact that the Prince d'Hénin, the titular "protector"

* E & J de Goncourt, *Sophie Arnould*, page 120

of Sophie Arnould, took a great antipathy to the
Chevalier de Gluck, and was extremely rude to
him, and also that Mlle ' Rosalie, the actress to
whom the parts were eventually given, was the
mistress of Comte Mercy d'Argenteau, the Austrian
Ambassador, whom Gluck, was particularly anxious
to oblige.

It would, however, be better to speak of these
matters in their proper chronological sequence.
Fortunately for the biographer, information about
Sophie at this time—the zenith of her career—
is more plentiful, Métra coming with his *Correspondance Secrète* to supplement his fellow scandal-monger,
Bachaumont. Neither is particularly trustworthy,
but if there is any choice between them, Bachaumont
is not only more complete, but is less malicious,
and does not seem to go out of his way—as
Métra continually does—to give some particularly
spicy lie about some living or dead person. *

The difference between them is but one of degree,
but is sufficient to make the reader of both veracious
historians conclude that, if they had lived in the
present day, Bachaumont would have found congenial
employment on the staff of one of the less reput-
able "society papers," whilst Métra would always
have been in Holloway Gaol, except when he was
in Dartmoor. Bachaumont's lies are rarely cruel,

* Métra's *Correspondance* is dated from London but no doubt was
written, printed, and published in Paris.

9

and are easily detected by any one with an average
amount of common sense. For instance, he starts
this year by giving on one of the first pages, under
date of January 20th, a couple of letters which are
stated to have passed between Sophie Arnould and
the Abbé du Terray. In the one, Sophie alludes
to the rumour that she is stated to have asked for
a *croupe*, or pecuniary interest in the farming of
one of the taxes, which *croupe* was supposed to
have been allotted her in recognition of her talents.
The Abbé replies that she has been misinformed,
but it is not necessary to quote the letters, for
they are obviously not genuine. The one is a
mere vehicle for getting in some digs at a very
unpopular Minister under cover of the name of the
witty, sarcastic actress; whilst the reply contains
some not over-decent quibbles concerning the notoriously immoral life which Sophie was known to be
leading.

If a guess might be hazarded as to the author-
ship of these letters, it would seem not unlikely that
if Comte de Lauraguais did not actually write them,
he had assisted to compose them, and if it be
urged that a gentleman was hardly likely to cast
reflections on a woman who had been his mistress
for several years and had borne him four children,
it may be replied that the code of honour in the
18th Century was very different to what it is now.

At any rate it is certain that about this time

that erratic and hot-tempered nobleman had returned to Paris after a more than usually long exile in England, during which he had made himself notorious in several ways. Perhaps he still had a secret hankering after Sophie, and would have liked to renew a *liaison* with one who was certainly dearer to him than his own wife, but his place had been taken, and for some time past the Prince d' Hénin had been the titular "protector" of Sophie.

The Prince does not appear to have been a very interesting individual. He was proud, pompous, priggish, and stupid, and not even the advantages of Sophie's society had succeeded in making him other than a bore. Perhaps Lauraguais had paid a visit to his old mistress, and found her changed, and he, being jealous of the Prince, or sorry to see Sophie linked, even temporarily, to such a dull, purse-proud companion, who was preferred before himself, resolved to play a practical joke on her protector.

Here is the story as given by Bachaumont.

" The Comte de Lauraguais, whose inextinguishable humour is so marvellously seconded by his lively imagination, after having amused London, has come to enliven our capital with his sallies and ingenious pleasantries, of which this is a charming instance.

He assembled four doctors of the Faculty of Medicine in consultation, to know whether it was possible for any one really to die of sheer *ennui*.

After a long discussion, they replied in the affirma-
tive, and signed a paper to that effect, they being
under the impression that the question related to
some member of the Comte's family, amongst whom
idiocy, hypochondria, and melancholia, were far from
infrequent.

The best remedy, they all agreed, would be "the
removal of the objects which caused this condition
of inertia and stagnation." This very obvious conclusion was exactly what the Comte desired. Having
obtained this valuable opinion, duly signed by the
four physicians, the Comte de Lauraguais went off
to a commissary of police, and gravely demanded
a warrant against the Prince d'Hénin, for reasons
which would be found in the subjoined written complaint. This document set forth that whereas the
Prince d'Hénin would, by his continual and weari-
some *obsession*, inevitably cause the death of Sophie
Arnould, whose life was precious to the public, and
more particularly so to him (the complainant), the
said Prince should be required or compelled to
abstain from visiting the aforesaid Demoiselle Arnould
until she had entirely recovered from the malady of
ennui by which she was attacked, and which in the
opinion of four eminent members of the faculty
would eventually kill her, unless the cause of her
complaint namely the society of the said Prince
d'Hénin was removed.

Of course the commissary did not issue any warrant, but he retold the story, and no doubt noted it down for the delectation of the King, who daily read all the police reports, and who would be sure to repeat to all his cronies this "charming instance of the inextinguishable humour" of Comte de Laura-guais. At any rate the story was soon all over Paris. Prince d'Ilénin was, not unnaturally, indignant, and talked about challenging the author of the practical joke; but the Prince's discretion was greater than his valour, it would appear, for more than once he was on the verge of fighting and then thought better of it.

The joke was not a bad one of its kind, and gained somewhat from the fact that Sophie was actually out of health at the moment, though she was not, perhaps, very seriously ill. Towards the end of January she was singing at the Opera, but early in February she was anxious to retire from the Stage, and did actually send in her resignation, but it was not accepted.

All the members of the Opera were regarded as being "His Majesty's servants" in the literal sense of the phrase. They enjoyed certain privileges, but they were not free agents, and having once taken service under the King were no longer their own masters. However young a girl might be, if she were once entered on the book of the Opera as belonging to the troupe, even her parents had no control over her. Dissipated young nobles took

advantage of this regulation, and if they wished to
abduct a young girl, first took the precaution of
getting her entered as a *danseuse* at the Opera.
When the elopement took place and the parents
appealed to the police to recover their erring daughter,
they would be informed, in the course of a day or
two, that she belonged to the Royal Opera, and
therefore was under no authority except that of the
King, or the gentlemen who formed the " Committee" which regulated the royal theatres.   This bad
business was put a stop to in 1775.

The answer vouchsafed to Sophie's application to
be released from her engagement was a polite
refusal, couched in the following terms.

"February 16, 1774.

" I am sorry to hear, Mademoiselle, that you are
thinking of retiring, on the ground that your weak
state of health does not permit you to fulfil your
duties as conscientiously as you would wish.   I
fully appreciate your honesty of purpose, but, at
the same time, I believe that at your age, and
with a little care, you may easily recover from your
indisposition, and therefore I am not prepared to
accept your proposal at present.   Several new works
are in preparation at the Opera, and as they are
not in your particular line of parts, you will be
able to enjoy a long rest; moreover, under no
circumstances would more be demanded of you

than your strength would permit. I am sure that you will not abuse this concession, but, on the contrary, it will act as a fresh incentive to make you assist, so far as it lies in your power, to support the welfare of the Academy."

Beneath these polite phrases and studied compliments there was, perhaps, a hint that the singer was only malingering. The writer made a shrewd guess that when Sophie tendered her resignation, professional jealousy and, perhaps, professional pride, had more to do with it than the state of her health. Sophie knew, as all the world did, that a new composer was about to introduce an entirely new school of opera. She was not by any means sure that she was suited to take leading parts in these operas (and, indeed, the official who wrote this letter seems to have been of opinion that her services would not be required) and she was greatly afraid that her younger, less-talented, and much-detested rival, Rosalie Levasseur, would be preferred before her. The Queen and the Court would warmly support the composer, so that it was almost a foregone conclusion that the Opera would be successful, and Sophie deemed it very probable that she would either be out of the cast altogether, and so have no share in the triumph, or be content with what small modicum of praise she could gain by playing second to Rosalie Levasseur.

It was very fortunate for Sophie Arnould that her resignation was not accepted. When the parts of *Iphigenia in Aulis* were distributed, Sophie was gratified to find that she was cast for *Iphigenia*, and there can be no doubt that Gluck made the best choice. He claimed that in his "musical dramas," music was to be the interpreter of poetry, and he hated everything that was insipid and artificial. Sophie Arnould, though her voice was not so fresh nor so powerful as that of her younger rival, was, without doubt, the greatest actress of the day, and the only singer whose genius could soar above the conventionalities which still hampered the operatic stage. Gluck may have known less counterpoint than Handel's cook, but he knew a great artiste when he came across one.

For her part she fully justified the confidence reposed in her. The opera, it was evident, would arouse public interest to an extent hitherto unknown. It is customary in France to admit many of the critics, the friends of the artistes and manager, and some privileged persons, to see the last, or dress, rehearsal of a new piece. The plan is not without some advantages, as it gives the critics plenty of time to write their critiques, and considerably reduces the quantity of "paper" in the house on the first night. In the present day it is not unusual, when an important piece is about to be produced, to find the house as full at the dress

rehearsal as it is at an ordinary performance, but
a hundred years ago there was not as a rule any
overweening amount of interest displayed in a new
opera or piece, and only a few melomaniacs were
present at the dress-rehearsal

With *Iphigenia*, however, the case was very different. Everyone desired to be present at one of
the rehearsals, and the managers and artistes were
overwhelmed with applications for admission. Such
crowds gathered round the theatre-doors that the
Provost of the Merchants consulted Rebel, the
manager, as to what was to be done. Rebel wrote
to Versailles for instructions, and received the following letter in reply.

"March 31, 1774.

"The Provost of the Merchants appears to fear,
and with some reason, that the rehearsals of the
opera of *Iphigenia* will be attended with some disturbances, on account of the enormous number of
people who have asked for tickets. No doubt it
would be desirable that the rehearsals should take
place with closed doors, or at least in the presence
of a few connoisseurs only. But I feel that it would be
very difficult at the present moment to act in opposition to public curiosity without exciting complaints on all sides. Precautions must be taken,
however, to prevent any disturbances, and to see
that the rehearsals take place quietly. The first is

to demand a guard of soldiers for each representation, the second is to give notice that no person will be allowed to enter without a ticket signed by one of the managers; the third to limit the admissions to the boxes to the number of persons that can be accommodated: the fourth, not to issue more than three or four hundred tickets for the pit, and one hundred for the gallery. By these means the rehearsals, it is to be hoped, will pass off quietly. I have written to the Provost of the Merchants, who wants several box seats, that he can ask you for as many as he requires. You would oblige also by reserving a box for M. de Villevault for the rehearsal on Saturday, and one for M. Joly de Fleury, a councillor, for the rehearsal on Monday. Both of them have asked me to procure them seats.

P. S. The public should only be admitted to the two last rehearsals; at all the others the doors ought to be tightly closed.

The rehearsals must have been amusing. Gluck had a good idea of stage-management, and was especially horrified at the chorus, which hitherto had been content to stand in a semi-circle, and perform its part without moving, or evincing the slightest interest either in the words it had to sing, or the action of the principal performers. The composer was anxious to make these singing-machines show some sign of human feeling, and he bustled about, putting the choristers into position, and teaching them how to act. The exertion made him so warm, that in a few minutes his coat would come off, and then his wig would follow. The spectacle of an elderly German gentleman darting about the stage in his shirt-sleeves, and with a cotton nightcap on his bald head must have been ludicrous enough, and was rendered more so by the conduct of some of his staunch admirers, who followed him about, carrying the articles of apparel he had thrown off

Nor were other amusing incidents wanting Mlle Duplant was really entitled to choose which part she would play, and she at once chose Iphigenia. This put Sophie Arnould in a difficulty. The part of Clytemnestra afforded the most scope for acting, or, in theatrical slang, had the most "fat," but on the other hand, Iphigenia was the "title rôle," and if she played Clytemnestra she would have to appear as the mother of an actress who was quite as old as herself. Mdlle. Duplant, for her part, was equally determined not to play the part of Mlle Arnould's mother. The difficulty was solved by a little diplomacy. To persuade Sophie to withdraw her claim would have been difficult if not impossible, and dread of her sharp tongue rendered it a task which no one was willing to undertake, so Madame Duplant was approached. She was persuaded that Sophie, on account of her many notorious gallantries would do justice to the love scenes, and Duplant finally accepted the part of Clytemnestra as a kind of testimonial to her comparatively superior morality.

Perhaps she was not quite as vicious as Sophie, but she was not a paragon of virtue. Her lover at this time was a certain M. Colin, a rich meat or cattle salesman. Sophie was, of course, aware of this, and was not improbably unacquainted with the arguments which had been used to persuade Duplant to accept the part of Clytemnestra. During one of the rehearsals a large dog strayed into the theatre, and found its way into the green-room. Sophie called the animal to her, patted it, and made friends with it, and then taking it by the collar led it on the stage, where Duplant was singing. Sophie went up to her, and pointing to the dog, parodied one of the lines in the opera and sang,

"Reine, de votre amant, voici l'ambassadeur"

All present laughed, and Mme. Duplant was covered with confusion.

Another amusing story related about these rehearsals is that at one point the chorus had to sing to Iphigenia :

"Rassurez-vous, belle princesse
Achille sera votre époux."

This was accompanied by the three notes D. E. C. on the horn. Sophie, for fun, hummed to these notes "Je m'en moque" or rather "Je m'en moo"— for she altered the word moque so as to rhyme with époux. It is not unlikely that the person who

Castel-Blaze—L. Académie impériale de musique.

reported this anecdote did not catch the words correctly, and that the Demoiselle Arnould made another rhyme to *époux*. The interpellation vastly tickled the large audience present at the rehearsal. Many of these persons were present at the first performance of the Opera, and when this point was reached, there were cries of "Louder! Louder!" The cry was repeated on subsequent occasions, and one night, "either by accident or design" the actress sang the words in a loud and intelligible voice.

Gluck's difficulties in getting *Iphigenia* properly rehearsed were increased by a royal decree, dated April 5th, 1774, which created much indignation, and it might almost be said consternation, amongst the "damsels of the Opera." By this decree "no person, unless connected with the theatre, was to be allowed to enter the green-room or the dressing-rooms of the actresses." The order was a sensible one, and much needed, and it must have afforded much satisfaction to Gluck to have the wings and the dressing-rooms cleared of intruders, but the measure was not due to his suggestion. It was due perhaps to a notary with the not inappropriate name of Bouby who had recently failed for 1,200,000 francs, which belonged to his clients. The whole of this large sum had been expended on the nymphs of the Opera, and the amorous notary was well known behind the scenes. The actresses guessed pretty correctly that the money he spent so freely did not all come out of his own pocket. "That poor pigeon has been nicely plucked," whispered a *danseuse* to Sophie Arnould one evening, pointing to the notary. "*Mais il peut voler, tout de même*," replied Sophie.

Iphigenia was to have been produced, on April 12th, but owing to the indisposition of M. Larrivée, the principal male-singer, the performance was postponed for a week, and the opera was produced on April 19th. The audience was perhaps the most brilliant that had ever assembled within the walls of the Opera-house. By half past five the Dauphin, the Dauphiness, and the Comte and Comtesse de Provence were already in the royal boxes, and the Duchesse de Chartres, Duchesse de Bourbon, Princesse de Lamballe, all the Ministers, and most of the Courtiers, had preceded them, and were waiting for the first notes of the overture. The overture was listened to with admiration, but the presence of the royal party prevented any manifestations of applause, until Marie Antoinette, at the close of Agamemnon's first recitative, gave the signal by clapping her hands, when thunders of applause burst forth from all parts of the house. The success of the opera was assured as far as the Court party was concerned, but, of course, as the Dauphiness warmly espoused the cause of Gluck, that was almost a foregone conclusion. The critics felt that, perhaps on that very account, *Iphigenia* was not likely to be well-received by the general public, and they discreetly "hedged," and confined themselves to giving a synopsis of the plot with a few words of praise to the principal performers. Sophie never acted better, and her voice seemed to have regained its strength, the *clou* of the opera being Agamemnon's air *Au faîte des grandeurs*, of which Abbé Arnoud said, "With that air one might found a religion."

The verdict of the public confirmed that of the Court, but the performances were interrupted owing to the death of the King which took place on May 10th. Madame du Barry was banished from Court, and Sophie Arnould said, in reference to herself and the other fair and frail damsels of the Opera: "We are orphans who have lost both father and mother." The artistes suffered a pecuniary loss, for the theatre was closed for some weeks, and only half salaries were paid during that time.

When the theatre reopened, the performances of *Iphigenia* were resumed, and became quite the rage. *Coiffures* in those days were enormous structures before which even the "matinée hat" might hide its diminished head. The coiffure *à l'Iphigénie* was comparatively a simple affair. It consisted of "a wreath of black flowers surmounted by the crescent of Diana, with a kind of veil which covered half the back of the head." * Sophie Arnould, of

* Metra, *Correspondance secrète* vol I, p. 64

course, wore one of these hats, and it became her
well " A respectable young woman," named Mme.
de Hunolstein, who lived in the Palais Royal, was
so fascinated by Sophie Arnould's acting in *Iphigenia*,
that she almost fell in love with her. How she
contrived to make her feelings known to the object
of her adoration, we cannot say, but Sophie presented her with one of these Iphigenia hats. Mme.
de Hunolstein found that she did not look quite as
pretty as the actress, and thinking that the hat
might have something to do with it, she sent the
new hat back to Sophie with a note requesting her
to change it for the one she wore. The lackey
who was sent with the hat and the message, was
ushered into Sophie's chamber, where he found the
hair-dresser arranging her hair. Prince d'Hénin was
also in the room; or, as Métra maliciously puts it,
Sophie had with her the lover who paid, and the
lover who was paid. She read the letter, and dis-
missed the lackey, then, taking the hat she usually
wore, she put it in a box, then looking from the
Prince to the barber, said gravely: " Whose turn
is it to run errands to day?"

    This was not the only occasion on which Sophie
showed her contempt for her protector. He was
continually getting snubbed, and seems often to have
deserved it. Gluck was then at work on a new
opera, *Orpheus and Eurydice*, and he often came to
Sophie's house, with some of the *artistes* of the

Opera, to try over some of the airs. These visits were particularly distasteful to Prince d'Hénin, who pretended to be jealous, and more than once he made sarcastic remarks about musicians in general and Gluck in particular The old composer took no notice of these observations for some time, but they rankled in his mind, and in future he only called on the *prima donna* at a time when she was likely to be alone. One day, when he and several of the singers were at Sophie's house trying over some of the music of *Orpheus*, Prince d'Hénin arrived unexpectedly, and entered the room. All rose from their seats and bowed—all except Gluck who settled himself more firmly on his chair, and took no notice of the Prince's entrance. The Prince was for a moment too astonished to do anything, but at last he said, "It seems to me that it is the custom in France to rise when anyone, and more especially a person of high position, enters."

Gluck bounded from his chair and came up to the Prince. "The custom in Germany, Monsieur," he replied, "is to rise if anyone you respect comes into the room—but not otherwise." Then turning towards Sophie Arnould, he added: "As you are not the mistress in your own house, I will leave, and will never return."

With that he stalked off home and proposed to send a challenge to the Prince, but reflected that it would be useless, as the Prince was a notorious

coward, and would inevitably take shelter behind his
rank, and refuse to fight with a musician even though
he were a Chevalier. Gluck therefore poured the story
of his wrongs into the ear of the Duc de Nivernais,
who was one of his warmest admirers. The Duc
immediately constituted himself the composer's champion and charged Prince d'Hénin with having insulted
Gluck at the house of Sophie Arnould, and insisted
that the Prince should either fight him (the Duc)
or apologise to Gluck. It is needless to say that
the Prince preferred the latter course, and duly
called upon the irate composer, and it is to be
presumed made the *amende honorable*, and settled
the matter amicably, for nothing more concerning
the quarrel is to be found in the writings of the
contemporary scandal-mongers.

CHAPTER IX.

PRINCE d'Hénin had really some cause for jealousy,
for Sophie Arnould had a "serious" lover, who was
deeply attached to her and whose affection endured
even to the time when she was old, ill, and poor.
This lover, whose name was François Joseph Belanger,
was an architect. Sophie Arnould made his ac
quaintance under the following circumstances. Mlle
Guimard, a *danseuse* of the Opera, who was one
of the most notorious and most extravagant *demi-
mondaines*, had a magnificent residence constructed
for her in the Chaussée d'Antin. This "temple of
Terpsichore," as it was called, had cost immense
sums, and had been the ruin of more than one of
the numerous lovers of the "skeleton of the Graces"
But Sophie also had rich lovers, and was jealous of
Mlle Guimard. She wanted to erect a palace
which should be even finer than that of the *danseuse*,

and Belanger was engaged to draw up the plans.
These were duly executed, and Sophie Arnould's
house still exists,—on paper, on the shelves of the
Bibliothèque Nationale. There are plans of the
ground, first, and second floors, the latter containing
four small rooms which Mlle Arnould had "*dem-
mandé*" (sic) to accommodate her children, and there
is a design for the façade, with an entablature supported by two caryatides, one of which was to be
the Muse Euterpe, whose lineaments were to be
those of Sophie herself. The building never got
beyond the paper stage, perhaps it would have
cost too much money, or perhaps Sophie, when she
fell in love with the architect, forgot all about the
projected palace.

Indeed François Joseph Belanger was just fitted
to captivate the affections of Sophie Arnould. He
was at this time a little over thirty years of age,
not bad looking, well-read, enthusiastic, good-tem-
pered, and an amusing companion. French architects,
even in the present day, often perform functions which
an English architect would deem derogatory to his
professional position, and Belanger, who was director
of the King's Menus Plaisirs, was not only called
upon to arrange the stage and the auditorium, but
also to engage the artistes. In his capacity of
entertainment caterer, he was of course acquainted
with all the artistes. He was therefore a welcome
guest at Sophie's supper parties, for, besides being

a good talker himself he often brought with him the latest novelty in the person of a new conjurer, juggler, or other performer of the same kind.   On one occasion for instance he brought with him to Sophie's house a conjurer, who declared that before the supper was over he would cause a large bust of the hostess which stood on a bracket in the room to disappear He performed a number of tricks, and wound up by calling the attention of the guests to the bracket, from which Sophie's bust had vanished, its place being taken by an object which need not be mentioned here.

As an architect, Belanger was one of the most rising men of the day.   He is mentioned in an Almanac of Architects, Artists, and Engravers, published in 1776, where his name occurs on the list of "Architects of Paris who have given proof of their talents," and he is described as "Inspector of Menus Plaisirs, Dessinateur de la Chambre et du Cabinet des Princes Frères du Roi," and his address is given as the Hôtel des Menus Plaisirs, Rue Bergère.   It stood a few yards to the east of where the Folie Bergère now is.   Belanger found his acquaintance with Sophie Arnould not only pleasant but profitable.   She recommended him to many of her friends or lovers, and so procured him a good deal of business.   His best works were the Villa and gardens of La Bagatelle, in the Bois de Boulogne, which he built and laid out for the Comte d'Artois, the stables, "surrounded by cottages in the English style," also built for Comte d'Artois, which stood where the Rue des Ecuries d'Artois now is; the Chateau de Méreville (Seine et Oise) built for the de la Tour du Pin family; the chateau of Bel Œil (Belgium) the seat of the Prince de Ligne. Extant specimens of his work are the hotel built for Mlle Contat at the corner of the Rue de Berri and the Champs Elysées, and the dome of the Old Corn Market (now the Bourse de Commerce) which is perhaps one of the earliest examples of the exclusive use of iron and glass in the construction of a cupola.

The affection was lasting, on his side at least; —on hers it was equally ardent for a short time at all events, but liable to interruption whenever she took a new fancy. Once when he was temporarily out of favour she wrote him a letter giving him his *congé*, and at the same time wrote to an actor named Florence inviting him to become her lover. Belanger chanced to call at Sophie's house at a time she was not at home and read these two letters and altered the addresses. Sophie appreciated a joke of that kind, and received him into favour again, the more readily perhaps, as Florence not being aware of the trick that had been played, ceased his visits. *

The incident is mentioned here to show Belanger's infatuation for Sophie Arnould. It must have taken place after her retirement from the stage, as Florence did not become a member of the Comédie Française till 1779.

Belanger was anxious to marry Sophie Arnould, but she refused him, though whether from selfish or unselfish motives, we cannot say. It may have been that she who had so played the queen on and off the boards, dreaded the sneers of her fellow actresses when it became known that she had married an architect; or it may be that she thought that his union with a notoriously depraved woman, who had three illegitimate children living, would ruin his career, and deprive him of the patronage of a severely moral King and Queen. If so he was only saved for a time. He remained unmarried for nearly twenty years, hoping possibly that Sophie Arnould would change her mind. Towards the close of the Revolution he was thrown into prison, and there met Mlle Dervieux, a noted courtesan. They were both lucky enough to save their heads, and he married her in prison. It did not prejudice him in the eyes of Louis XVIII at any rate, for after the Restoration he was made a Chevalier of the Legion of Honour—and at that time the Order was not bestowed so freely as it now is—and was appointed to several important posts.

Perhaps both reasons had something to do with Sophie's refusal, and the first in a greater degree than the second. But though they were never married, it was rumoured that they were, and Sophie was twitted with having thrown herself away upon an architect. "So many stones are cast at me," replied the witty actress, "that I thought an architect would be the best man to utilize them."

It is time, however, that we should return to the history of Sophie. In August, 1774, Gluck produced his second opera, *Orpheus and Eurydice*, and Sophie Arnould was entrusted with the part. She did not avail herself of the opportunity to the same extent that she had done in *Iphigenia*, though the *Mercure* said she displayed "much soul, intelligence, and precision," and the honours of the evening rested with Le Gros. The general impression created by the opera was that the music was very fine, but that the author of the libretto had "abused his privilege of being common-place"* and the ballets were not half so good as the ballets in *Castor*, an old opera by Rameau first played in 1737, and reproduced several times in the succeeding years. A mild joke circulated in the pit to the effect that *Orpheus* was only a *demi-castor*,—a term used to designate a kind of hat, and also applied to loose women of the lower order.

Before the end of the year a very bad production was brought out—an opera entitled *Azolan*, by a very mediocre musician named Floquet. Up to this time it had been usual for the orchestra to play during the *entr'actes*, but Gluck introduced the custom of giving the musicians a well deserved rest. The composer of *Azolan* thought he could not do better

* Grimm's *Correspondance*, vol. X, p. 472.

than follow Gluck's example, which caused one of the violinists to say that "the only good things in *Azolan* were the *entr'actes*, and those were Gluck's."

The Comte d'Artois was a constant attendant at the Opera, and though he had been married not quite a year, was said to be very susceptible to the charms of the "nymphs" of the ballet. M. Castel Blaize states that in the November of this year, he compelled the City of Paris to give him one of the boxes which belonged to the Municipality, and his first care was to have green blinds fitted to it so that the audience could not see him or the other occupants, and that one night " he conducted thither in a mysterious manner, Madame du Barry, who was almost old enough to be his grandmother." * For the sake of M Castel Blaize's reputation as a historian, it is to be hoped that most of his statements are more correct than this one. Whoever accompanied Comte d'Artois it was certainly not Madame du Barry, who was then strictly confined in the Abbaye of Pont-aux-Dames, and was not released till a year later. She would also, it may be remarked, have been an extremely youthful grandmother for she was only thirty-one years of age at this time!

A few words must be said, before we terminate the account of this year, about the quarrel between Sophie Arnould and Mlle Raucourt, of the Comédie

* *L'Académie Impériale de musique*, Paris, 1885

Française. The latter was a young woman who appeared before Louis XV in 1772, and had so pleased that monarch that he had given orders she was to be admitted into the company of the Théâtre Français. She had also succeeded in winning the good graces of Madame du Barry, by pretending that she was born in the same part of the country as the King's Favourite, and also that her father had been one of the actors in the private troupe of Stanislas, King of Poland. The first part of the statement was not true, for she was born in Paris;* and though the latter part probably was—for she was a true *enfant de la balle*—she would not perhaps have mentioned the matter if she had not been aware that Madame du Barry's uncle was a footman in the household of the same monarch.

Mlle Raucourt was not quite seventeen when she was accepted as a member of the Comédie Française, and was at that time a "dragon of virtue," and had vowed always to remain chaste and virtuous. She became acquainted with Sophie Arnould, and even reproved the elder actress for her way of living, and pointed out the advantages of chastity and modesty.

"That may be so," replied Sophie, "but I have read in the Bible of a certain fig tree that was cursed, and withered away—and only because it was a virgin."

So M Jal asserts. *Duc. Critique de Biog.,* p 1042.

It is sad to say that Mlle Raucourt's virtuous resolves soon vanished, and she evinced an amount of depravity which only Sophie Arnould and one or two others could have hoped to equal. The friendship between the two women soon turned cold, and then degenerated into open enmity. Indeed when we consider that Mlle Raucourt was hardly more than half Sophie's age, was very pretty and had shown a remarkable aptitude in acquiring the vices of the *demi-mondaine*, it seems obvious that neither would be likely to brook a rival near her throne, and their mutual hate can be easily explained without recourse to the theories which the scandal-mongers of the day were not ashamed to put forth, or MM. E. & J. de Goncourt to repeat.

Each began to say spiteful things about the other, and, as might have been expected, the younger actress was no match for the elder in sarcasm. A young and pretty woman, who is free with her favours, will, however, never lack champions, and if they were no match for Sophie in wit, they could make up for it in abuse, or even exchange a sword thrust or two with Sophie's admirers.

The Marquis de Villette, who was one of Mlle Raucourt's faction, once expressed himself rather strongly about Sophie Arnould; Belanger, Sophie's lover, chanced to be present, and took her part warmly, whereupon the Marquis declared that he would "smash any rascal who dared to contradict him." Belanger understood this to mean that the lackeys of the Marquis would cudgel him, and he claimed the protection of the police. Then the friends of both parties interfered, and the quarrel was settled in a manner that would have delighted Touchstone. The opponents were to meet sword in hand, and then were to be separated before they had time to do each other any harm. This little comedy was played out seriously enough, and honour was declared to be satisfied on both sides.

In the early days of January, 1775, *Iphigenia in Aulis* was revived. Gluck had made several additions and alterations in the score, and, very much against his will, had lengthened the ballets Indeed he seemed so willing to oblige anybody and everybody, that old Vestris asked him to insert a *chaconne* for the younger Vestris to dance.

"Do you think the Greeks danced the *chaconne?*" growled the composer.

"Didn't they?" asked the old dancer in honest amazement; "then they were greatly to be pitied."

"Well, well!" said the Chevalier, "you shall have your *chaconne*, though *the opera stinks of music already.*"

Nevertheless old Vestris obtained his *chaconne*, and *Iphigenia* was even more rapturously received than on its first production All the *artistes* resumed their old parts, and with even greater success than ever—at least so said those critics who were Gluckists.

On January 13th, Marie Antoinette, accompanied by Monsieur, Madame, and the Comte d'Artois, came to see the opera. The Queen sent for the Chevalier Gluck, and complimented him on the success of his work. Some lines of flattery, addressed to the Queen, had been added to the part of Achilles, and produced an outburst of enthusiasm when they were recited by Le Gros.

As usual, Sophie did not appear after the first few performances, and the part of *Iphigenia* was taken by Mlle Laguerre, who had previously scored a success as *Eurydice*. But in March, Mlle Laguerre pleaded illness, and gave up the part to Rosalie Levasseur. "Peste!" said Sophie, "for a *débutante* this young person gives herself a great many airs. She is already indisposed—just as though she were a prima donna."

Mlle Laguerre though a *débutante* in the musical profession was no novice in vice. Young as she was she was utterly depraved, and her extravagance knew no bounds. The Duc de Bouillon spent upon her 800,000 francs in three months. During her illness, someone asked Sophie if Mlle Laguerre was better. "Poor girl, she is still very ill," replied Sophie, "and lives on nothing but Bouillon."

It may reasonably be doubted whether there was anything very serious the matter either with Mlle Laguerre or Mlle Arnould. At any rate, Sophie was at the Théâtre Français on one of the most me-

morable nights in the history of French stage—the
23rd of February when *The Barber of Seville* was first
produced. She had no very great admiration for
Beaumarchais personally, and much under-estimated
his undoubted talent. She regarded him rather as
a lucky rogue who could palm off his brass as gold.
"He will live to be hanged,—but the rope will
break," she once said of him. But she fully appreciated the satire of the *Barber*, much of the wit
of which was akin to her own. When some one
said that the piece "fell flat," Sophie replied, "If
so it will fall fifty times in succession."

The success of the *Barber* was soon assured, and
the directors of the Opera must have wished that
they could have found a work that would prove
equally attractive, for though the Gluckites filled the
house whenever *Iphigenia* was performed, on the
other nights business was very bad. As a last
resort, *Procris et Céphale* was produced in May.
That very considerable doubt was felt as to its reception in Paris was pretty evident from the fact
that though most new operas were produced in Paris
within a few days or weeks after they had been
first tried at Versailles, nearly eighteen months had
elapsed since *Procris et Céphale* was performed before
Louis XV ere it made its appearance on the Paris
boards. The King had not been able to sit out
the performance, but there was nothing remarkable
about that, as everything bored him, and nothing

but a pretty actress could induce him to witness more than one or two acts, and under any circumstances he left after the third act.

Procris was in five acts, but the authors judiciously cut it down to four when it was being prepared for the Paris stage. But though the authors had, as Sophie said, "put themselves *en quatre* in order to please the public," the opera was a dismal failure, and was "severely judged" by the critics. This was namely due to the libretto which was written by Marmontel. He had unfortunately introduced an occasional Latin word, and this was greatly resented by the public. In one scene the word *aura* occurred whereupon a wit in the pit called out, "*Ora pro nobis*," and that very mild pun settled the fate of the opera. Sophie Arnould declared that the music of *Céphale* was far more French than the words.* As is almost always the case, composer and librettist each charged the other with being the sole cause of the failure of their joint-work. *Céphale* was withdrawn after a few representations and *Orphée* revived, until a novelty was ready.

The novelty was not, however, of a nature to attract the public. Marie Antoinette had asked Gluck to compose an opera on a subject she should choose, and of course such a request was equivalent to an order, and Gluck at once professed his readiness to do whatever he was asked, though he had

* Grétry, the composer, was born at Liège

serious misgivings about the choice being a suitable
one. His fears were well-founded, for the Queen
selected *Cytherea Besieged*, a light opera-ballet in
three acts, by Favart. A worse choice it would
have been hard to make. Gluck's genius was sombre
and mournful, what talent Favart possessed was light
and playful. It was like harnessing a dray-horse to
a child's cart. Any *habitué* of the Opera would at
once have predicted that such an ill-assorted pair
could not possibly work together with any chance
of success

The new opera was written, and produced on
August 1st, 1775. When the curtain went up, the
male chorus rushed on the stage, dressed as *abbés*,
and some of them carrying short ladders. "What
are the ladders for?" asked someone in the
audience. "To put up the posters for a new
opera," replied Sophie, who was sitting in one
of the boxes. The ladders were placed against
a rampart on "the King's" side of the stage,
and the abbés began to mount, but then there
appeared on the wall a host of young women
in low-necked dresses, who repulsed the enemy
"*avec des armes blanches*," as some one wittily said,
by throwing flowers.* It was just such a scene as
Favart or Voisenon might have been expected to
put on the stage, or Boucher, or Fragonard, to
have painted, but all the while it was being enacted,

* Castel Blaze *L'Académie Royale*, vol. 1, p. 337.

the orchestra was playing airs which would not
have been inappropriate accompaniments to the woes
of Clytemnestra, or the grief of Orpheus. "Her-
cules," said Sophie Arnould, "is more used to handle
the club than the spindle." The anti-Gluckists,
of course, declared that the failure of the opera was
due to the "monotonous and sad music," whilst
Gluck's party maintained that the work would have
been successful but that it was badly rendered.
This could hardly have been true, for "never had
a piece been prepared, rehearsed, and mounted
with so much care" *

In spite of royal patronage and careful mounting,
Cytherea was a failure, and was quickly withdrawn,
and some new *Fragments*, produced the following
month, met with no better success. What with
bad houses, and two of the leading lady artistes—
Sophie Arnould and Laguerre—not available, the
position of the managers was not enviable. Laguerre
had been temporarily removed from the stage by
the Duc de Bouillon. It was, apparently, a tradition in his family that they should always choose
their mistresses from the Opera. "It is said,"
cynically remarked the Duc, "that our race has
degenerated, and that we are not worthy descendants
of Godfrey de Bouillon. That is an error or a
calumny. You see that I adore Laguerre, my father
loves Victoire, and my son cares for nothing but

* Annales Dramatiques, vol iii, p 58

Bataille." Laguerre had the reputation of being the most extravagant woman of the day, or at least shared that distinction with a Mlle Cléophile, a *danseuse* who was the mistress of the Spanish Ambassador. There were several others who ran them very close in this respect. One of them—Mlle Granville—afforded Louis XVI an opportunity of displaying his sense of justice. She had wheedled bills for 300,000 francs out of a *maître des requêtes* named Jonville Before the bills became due he repented of his liberality, and brought a charge against the actress, before the Lieutenant of Police, that the money had been wrongfully extorted from him. The Lieutenant thought it was too big a case for him, and referred the matter to the Duc de la Vrillière. In the days of Louis the Well-beloved, the Duc would have experienced no difficulty in settling the affair. He would have ascertained which of the two parties was willing to pay the more to have the other locked up, and would have acted accordingly. Either the actress or the *maître des requêtes* would have been put in the Bastille until she or he was willing to forego or settle the claim. But, under Louis XVI, *lettres de cachet* were dull upon a falling market, and there was even a Prime Minister who was so inconsiderate as to go to the prisons, question the prisoners, and let out those against whom there appeared to be no case.

The Duc therefore declined to judge the affair, and

suggested that the King was the only person capable of settling such a knotty point. The case was laid before Louis XVI, and his decision, which was eminently characteristic of him, is described by one French writer as "iniquitous and stupid." Jonville must pay the 300,000 francs, he decided, because the money had been honestly earned; but as Mlle Granville was a depraved woman who caused the financial and physical ruin of many of the King's loyal subjects, she should be sent to prison as a common strumpet. This decree was duly obeyed, or at all events the latter part of it was, and Mlle Granville was sent to prison, and her hair, which was exceedingly long and beautiful, was cut off.

It is very unlikely that Mlle Laguerre received any salary during her absence, and indeed, if she had run away with a commoner instead of with a duke, she would probably have been put in prison for a short time. But Sophie Arnould claimed her salary on the ground that she was only prevented from acting by illness. The managers had suggested giving her a fixed sum for each night she played, but the proposal made her very indignant. That she really had been ill about this time appears evident from a letter still extant addressed to her notary, M. Alleaume, and which is dated July 3rd, 1775. It is the first glimpse we catch of those terrible money-troubles from which she was never to be free.

"Bonjour donc, mon bon ami. I have just come

from the country where I have been at grass for a
month, after having been two months on milk; all which
has restored the worthy Sophie to health. At present
I am almost well and am thinking about putting in order
my domestic affairs—in which you also take some interest; if it is not making too great a demand on your
kindness towards me, I would ask you to give me an
account of the present condition of my affairs.

" Come and see me, my good friend; come, that
I may kiss you heartily on both eyes without laughing

" SOPHIE."

July 3rd, 1775.

Towards the end of October, the managers
proposed to mount *Adèle de Ponthieu*, but Bachaumont
suggested that Sophie Arnould was getting too old
to play the part, and doubted whether her facial
expression and worn-out voice would compensate
the public for the loss of Mlle Laguerre whose
pretty face and clear voice still lingered in the
memory of the *habitués* of the Opera. Her admirers,
however, might console themselves with the reflection
that, thanks to the Duc de Bouillon, the actress,
was enjoying a considerable revenue, and would
probably retire. What satisfaction they were to derive
from that is not very evident, unless their admiration
took a very unselfish form. Perhaps if we could
get a glimpse of Bachaumont's cash book or private
diary, we might find a key to this and many
another puzzling paragraph

Three days later he speaks of the production of
some "Fragments," whilst *Idile* was being prepared,
and believes that when that opera is given, Sophie
will be paid by *cachet*, that is to say a fixed price
for each representation, though she had previously
refused that arrangement. There were four separate
acts, in one of which Sophie Arnould appeared with
moderate success, the chief honour of the evening
resting with Sieur Le Gros. One unfortunate actress,
Mlle Chateauneuf, was hooted and hissed until she
became quite ill, but was nevertheless compelled to
finish her part. She attributed her disgrace to Rosalie
Levasseur, whom she accused of having organised
a conspiracy against her. The two had a quarrel
and even came to blows. They also "nagged" at
each other on the stage, much to the delight of the
young aristocrats in the boxes, but at length they
settled their dispute by finding a common ground
of agreement and sympathy in the fact that Sophie
Arnould was paid five louis for each performance,
which they both joined in considering as much more
than she was worth. To pay such a salary, they
said, was "to reward idleness that ought rather to be
punished." "The amateurs," says Bachaumont, "are
much disquieted and do not know how it will all end."

These amateurs appear—in the pages of this
chronicler at least—to have been a curious body
of men and women. They could console themselves
for the disappearance of Mlle Laguerre by the

reflection that their favourite actress was engaged in the congenial employment of spending 800,000 francs in three months, but they could severely repress any conduct which evinced disrespect, either to themselves or to the Royal Family. Early in December, *Adèle de Ponthieu* was produced, and Sophie might have scored a great success, but for an unforeseen circumstance. The young Duc d'Artois was present, in the box which he had cajoled or bullied the City of Paris into giving him, and which he had fitted up with an elaborate system of screens and blinds, so that the occupants of the box could not be seen by the audience. Though very young, and only just married, he had the reputation of being very "fast" and it is not improbable that from the depths of this very private box he made signs to the actress, for she nodded and smiled at him, "exactly as she would have done to a comrade or a lover," says the deeply shocked Bachaumont. The public also was horrified at this display of familiarity, and "testified its indignation in a way that was humiliating to her."

Thanks partly to her poverty, and partly to her ready wit, Sophie Arnould lived through all the stormy days of the Revolution, but it is curious to reflect that if she had ever been denounced as a "suspect," Fouquier Tinville would have made out of the incident just mentioned a case against her more than sufficient to send her to the guillotine.

CHAPTER X.

(1776)

SOPHIE ARNOULD must often have felt, even before
1776, that her stage career was virtually over, and
her fears on this subject were fully confirmed in the
April of that year, when Gluck's opera of *Alceste*
was produced for the first time, and the principal
character was entrusted to Mlle Rosalie Levasseur.

The blow was the heavier since Sophie had a
double claim; she was not only the better artiste,
but she was the senior *prima donna*, and could
therefore claim any part she chose in any new opera
or reproduction.

It was open to the manager or the composer to
break through this tradition, and one or both of
them did so on this occasion. Gluck had, perhaps,
not forgotten his encounter with the Prince d'Hénin,
and though he was no longer Sophie's protector,
Gluck may possibly have borne malice against her.

But he had also a more powerful motive. He was
an Austrian subject, and the Austrian Ambassador
at that period was Comte de Mercy Argenteau, and
Rosalie Lavasseur was the Comte's mistress. In the
days of Louis XV, a mistress was almost as integral
a portion of an Ambassador's suite as a secretary
Apparently it was thought to lend an added lustre
to the dignity of a King, Emperor, or Empress that
his or her representative should be known as the
lover *en titre* of some popular singer or dancer.
Besides, such a *liaison* afforded the readiest means
for that lavish expenditure which an Ambassador
deemed needful in order to keep up the *prestige* of
the Court he represented. If he bestowed large sums
on the poor, or gave handsome presents or rich
entertainments to the courtiers, it might have been
thought that he was undermining the loyalty of either
class and he could not always rely on losing at the
gaming table, but a fashionable mistress was not
only capable of spending enormous sums, but also
of letting it be known that she did spend them, and
whence she procured them.

Louis XVI would probably have cared very little
either way, or perhaps preferred that the Ambassadors should not cause open scandals, but the custom
endured down to the Revolution. Comte de Mercy
Argenteau was certainly not the sort of man to
break through a rule of this sort. For the last three
or four years of the late King's life he had been

sedulously employed in trying to persuade the proud
and haughty Marie Antoinette to show some polite-
ness or consideration for Madame du Barry. He
had to gloze over to his Imperial Mistress the conduct of the Princess, coax promises of future good
behaviour out of the latter, persuade the Favourite
that any rebuffs she received must be construed in
a Pickwickian sense, and keep from the King the
knowledge of any slight being offered to the Du
Barry, and a particularly hard time he seems to
have had of it. If Madame du Barry had been an
exacting or imperious woman, his position would
have been simply untenable, but, luckily for him, she
was of a singularly sweet and gentle disposition.

Perhaps it was that having spent so much time
and eloquence in trying to persuade Marie Antoinette
that it was rather praiseworthy than otherwise to
keep a mistress that he felt bound to act up to his
principles, or perhaps he was actuated by the reasons
previously given, but it may certainly be imagined
that considering his advanced age, and the daily
and hourly anxiety that he had endured for years
on account of one improper female, that he was
likely to eschew the society of women of that kind
for the rest of his life.

At any rate, whether from personal or political
motives we know not, he became the acknowledged
protector of Rosalie Levasseur, and she not only
squandered his money right royally, but teased and

bullied him most thoroughly. She insisted that
Gluck should be her singing-master, and the old musician was accommodated in her house.

Nearly everybody was more or less of a toady
in those days, and Gluck was certainly not free from
that charge, and thought he could not better display his devotion to his country than by doing
whatever the Ambassador wished. Rosalie took
advantage of this, and began by insisting that Gluck
should be given an apartment in her house in order
that she might receive singing-lessons from him.
She thus managed to get him to teach her the
music of *Alceste*, and then hinted pretty plainly that
he ought to entrust her with the part when the opera
was produced. She pointed out that her voice was
fresher and more powerful than that of Sophie
Arnould—which was undeniably true—and though
she might lack the dramatic force of the elder
actress, she would play the part exactly as the composer wished, whereas Sophie would very likely insist
upon her own reading.

These arguments were successful, and Rosalie was
promised that she should be allowed to create the
part of *Alceste*. Sophie Arnould was, perhaps,
disappointed, but certainly not surprised. She knew
that Gluck was living in the hotel of her rival, and
that it was certainly not for his good looks that he
had been housed there, and she knew, of course,
what all Paris knew, that Comte Mercy Argenteau

was the "protector" of Mlle Rosalie Levasseur. There had never been any love lost between the two artistes, for they had hardly one attribute in common except unchastity, and even that differed in kind, for Sophie was capable of affection, whereas Rosalie was utterly heartless and mercenary, according to all accounts.

One of the very few instances in which they did agree, happened at this very time. Ever since the death of Rebel, the late manager, the affairs of the Opera had been in a bad way. M. Malesherbes, the Minister, who ought to have appointed a new manager, was busy with far more important affairs, and, moreover, unwilling to assume control over an institution which was more troublesome than profitable. For almost identical reasons— coupled with the fact that, whenever there was anything worth seeing, the junior members of the Royal Family occupied all the best boxes, and did not pay for them—the City of Paris refused to undertake the management of the Royal Academy of Music; the consequence being that the responsible post of *impresario* was left open to competition. Several individuals and syndicates offered to take over the management of the Opera, and at the head of one of these latter was the Chevalier de St. Georges.

The Chevalier has left some slight mark in history—principally owing to the fact that he has been made the hero of a fairly successful novel. He was at this time about thirty years of age, and was renowned for his proficiency in fencing and athletic exercises He was also an amateur musician, and well known in society; but he was born at Guadeloupe, and had a considerable quantity of black blood in his veins. The syndicate or association of which he was the nominal head contained several influential persons, and it was therefore generally believed that the Chevalier would be appointed manager of the Opera.

Thereupon, the lady artistes of the Opera, drew up a petition and sent it to the Queen. It was signed by Sophie Arnould, Rosalie Levasseur, Mlle Guimard, and others, and was to the effect that these respectable ladies would feel themselves " wounded in their honour and delicacy if they had to serve under the orders of a mulatto." The Queen, who, no doubt, knew the character of the signatories, was possibly of the opinion of Lady Teazle, that it might have been as well to leave honour out of the argument, but, at any rate, the Chevalier did not get the post he coveted. The difficulty was settled by the King announcing that he would appoint a manager at a fixed salary, and if at the end of the year there was any deficit in the budget, he would make it good out of his privy purse, but that if there were any profits they should be divided between those artistes who had received the greatest applause during the year.

Poor Sophie Arnould must have seen in the selection of Rosalie Levasseur for the part of *Alceste* the end of her own dramatic career. When she heard the news she contented herself with re-marking, "Rosalie ought to have the part; she has the voice of the people."

The satire was not very keen, but it sufficed to put the excitable Rosalie into a terrible temper. She was quite well aware that she was no match for Sophie in repartee, so she engaged one of her admirers to write a lampoon, and a copy of this precious production was sent to Sophie, and a few others shown in the green-room of the Opera, or sent to friends or admirers of Mlle Arnould. A more vulgar and disgusting production was never penned. If some fifty years ago, an Oxford under-graduate had put to the Thames bargee the most gifted in language, the time-honoured query concern-ing the kitten and Marlow Bridge, he would have received in reply much such a torrent of abuse, but there would have been a spice of originality and humour about the harangue, and the bargee would never have addressed it to a woman.

Sophie was perhaps annoyed by this coarse and insulting screed, but she effectually turned the tables on the author and instigator of the insult by sending her copy to the papers. It was of course published, and as is usually the case, disgusted all who read it, including even Bachaumont and Pidansat de

Mairobert, and procured Sophie many friends, and her rival many enemies.

Alceste was produced on April 23rd, 1776, and though well received, seems not to have been such a startling success as either *Iphigenia* or *Orpheus*. At least it was not so much appreciated by the general public. The Gluckists declared that only idiots could fail to recognise in the opera the greatest work of the greatest composer the world had ever known. The Bailli du Rollet said that "the music was the most passionate, energetic, and dramatic that had ever been heard in any European theatre since the art of music was created," but he was not altogether a disinterested critic, being the author of the libretto !

Rosalie Levasseur played intelligently, although her face and figure were not suited for tragedy, and the general, and no doubt correct, impression was that Sophie Arnould would probably have looked and played the part better, but not sung it so well.

In spite of all diversities of opinion, *Alceste* was sufficiently successful to run for several months, with occasional performances of other operas. *Adèle de Ponthieu* was now and then given, and Sophie Arnould sang in it—sometimes at least. A ballad, quoted *in extenso* by Grimm, makes out that Rosalie was jealous of the success achieved by the tenor, Larrivée, in this opera, and she is represented in the song as complaining to Comte Mercy Argenteau, that "Arnould may be left alone, for she is hardly any longer liked, Le Gros may bray to his heart's content, but Larrivée is the pet of the pit," and asking her protector to restore her waning popularity. If the ballad is to be trusted, Comte Mercy delighted his mistress by removing this difficulty in a manner which was quite according to the diplomacy of the day. He paid Larrivée 25 louis on condition that he did not sing his best. The bribe does not seem a heavy one, but salaries were not large in those days.

Rosalie did not keep the part very long. Three weeks later it was given to Mlle Laguerre, which Bachaumont thinks must have "redoubled the rage of Mlle Arnould," but that is doubtful. She had a great deal of professional pride, and it may be questioned whether she would have accepted a part that had been played by one she regarded as her inferior. Mlle Laguerre delighted her admirers, and had the additional merit of being very pretty. She was of very humble birth, and it was rumoured that her father and mother were both street-hawkers. He sold songs, and she sold a sort of cake known as "*plaisir des dames*," which afforded Sophie an opportunity for getting off one of her characteristically spiteful remarks.

By the anti-Gluckists, Sophie Arnould was regarded as a kind of champion. They ignored the obvious reasons for her being passed over, and professed to believe that she had refused to appear in any opera that was not French, ignoring the fact that she had already won success in the works of the German composer. The effect of this ill-abused partisanship was to prejudice the powerful party of the Gluckists still more against her.

On the off nights, when stock operas were played, Sophie's friends assembled in numbers, and applauded her to their hearts' content. It was but seldom that she was in good voice, and the Gluckists declared that she could not sing because she was too old. One of the few critics still friendly to her, Lefuel de Mercourt, took up her defence, and wrote in his journal, _Le Nouveau Spectateur_—a theatrical journal of the period——

"We know nothing concerning the age or the place of birth of this actress, who has long been, and still is, one of the great attractions of the Opera, where she plays emotional parts with the greatest success. Many persons have accused her of being ill-natured, but others who are worthy of credence, and who know her, have assured us that she is good-hearted, though rather satirical, and has plenty of sense. She is almost the Ninon of our age. She gathers round her men of all sorts and conditions provided only they are witty—and in that respect differs greatly from her comrades, who are incapable of distinguishing a polished gentleman from a brute."

The compliment was a clumsy one at the best,

but compliments of any sort were becoming rare,
and Sophie acknowledged it—in the following letter.

" I can but thank you, Sir, for the kind remarks
you have put in your paper concerning my poor
talents and me personally. I should deem myself
but too fortunate if the public would show me the
same indulgence that you have, and would do
justice to the efforts I have always made to please
it and merit its kindness.

" You preserve silence as to my age: were you
afraid of hurting my feelings in speaking of a subject which is a delicate matter with all my sex?
Do not alarm yourself—it is no secret, or only a
stage one at the most. Though it matters little so
long as I can play my parts conscientiously, I still
desire to preserve, in the theatre at least, that illusion
of youth which theatrical popularity always ensures;
for the public regards actresses as Cupid does
soldiers—and he cares but little for an old soldier

" But—out of mere coquetry, perhaps—I will con-
fide in you. I was born the 14th of February, 1744,
in the parish of St Germain-l'Auxerrois, in the
same room in which Admiral Coligny was murdered.
That is the only interesting circumstance connected
with my birth with which I am acquainted. As is
well known, I made my first appearance in the
month of December, 1757 Anyone who can cal-
culate that eight and eight make sixteen, will also

12

be able to find out that sixteen and sixteen make thirty-two. *

"I await inpatiently your criticisms on the opera of *Alcestes* which is about to interest, and perhaps divide, all Paris. Your opinion will confirm that which I was able to form from seeing the rehearsals only. If the success I achieved in *Iphegenia* prepossessed me favourably in regard to the authors, their want of consideration for me—I might even say their bad conduct towards me—must have served to change my opinion of them; but I have too much self-respect (although those gentlemen may not believe it) to join in any cabals or plots against the new work. Such proceedings I have always considered beneath me—they savour either of buffoonery or spitefulness. The only revenge I have taken was not to assert my right to the principal part, but no personal quarrel shall make me ignore the claims of genius, or prevent me from doing justice to the genius of Gluck. He is, I boldly affirm, the musician of the soul, and knows how to express in music all the feelings and passions, more especially sadness and grief.

"As to the author of the words, I leave him to the judgment of the public. If I belonged to the French Academy I might add my criticism to those

* Sophie, it should be remarked, does not say that she was only 32, though she leaves it to be implied. In reality she had knocked four years off her age, for she was born February 14th, 1740, not 1744, as she here states.

of the Forty—but I only belong to the Academy of Music. I acknowledge my incompetence and preserve silence, but I might observe that subjects as interesting as *Iphigenia*, and models as sublime as Racine, are not always to be found.

"If I may be allowed to say anything in regard to the performers, I should praise the acting of M. Gros as *Admetus*, and the singing of Mlle Rosalie as *Alcestis*.

"I have the honour to be, etc.,

Sophie Arnould."

The friendly journalist took Sophie's part, and in reviewing *Alcestes* said, or permitted an anonymous correspondent to say, that "the opera was sung by invalids who seemed to have taken half a pint of emetic and to be making vain efforts to vomit," and he asks if that is the proper way to "jaw" the sublime poem of Signor Calzabigi ?

In the next number, another writer, or the same, reproved Gluck for "having chosen a girl like Rosalie to play the part of Alcestes," and wound up by plaintively asking "Was there not the demoiselle * * *?"—the three stars no doubt standing for Sophie Arnould. A little later, there appeared in the same journal, a paragraph to this effect.

"I intend to see again that rather mournful, but not very affecting, opera, *Alcestes*, if only to confirm my opinion as to the superiority of Demoiselle * * * over

the rival that M. Gluck wrongly preferred before
her through ignorance of the taste of the nation
both in music and in acting."

There is also an allusion to a claim that Sophie
Arnould had made against the managers of the
Opera. Her business man is said to have presented
a note showing that as she had gained credit in
every part she had ever sustained there was a large
balance due to her.

The unfortunate man of business, the notary,
Alleaume, was not likely to have bothered his head
with any fancy claim, for the real affairs of Mlle
Arnould already occasioned him trouble enough.
We have already quoted one of the letters addressed
to him, and here give another from the packet
recently discovered by M. Henry Gauthier-Villars
and published by him in *La Nouvelle Revue* (February, 1897). The others which form this interesting collection will be given under their proper dates.
This letter is not dated, but appears to have been
written some time during the winter of 1775—76.

"Will you please, my dear Alleaume, advance me
my month, that is to say, my friend, give me 50 louis.
Apropos of money, I ran about all yesterday morning
to get some to send to you from the Prince de Conty,
and also from the Prince de Condé The weather is
too bad for me to go about this morning after it,
but to-morrow I will try to finish the job to your
satisfaction. I shall have, my friend, to remit you,

From the Prince de Conty 4250 frs.

From the Prince de Condé 3250 „

Mlle Desmarque's rent   1250 „

. We may guess from this that Sophie still received
a yearly allowance from at least two of herrich
and aristocratic lovers. How long these annuities
lasted we do not know, but they seem to have
come to an end very soon, and perhaps the in-
stalments just cited were the last.

For the next five months (May to October 1776)
we hear nothing of Sophie. Whether she had been
sulking all the time, or whether she continued to
appear occasionally in stock operas, we cannot
say. On October 1st of this year she sang the part
of *Lyris* in a little opera entitled *Euthyme et Lyris;*
words by Boutellier, and music by a very mediocre
musician, named Desormery. *Lyris* was the last
original part created by Sophie Arnould.* Desormery had previously tried three or four small
operas, all of which had been signal failures. His
Euthyme, however, met with considerable success,
and was played 26 times—an exceedingly good run
in those days. This exceptional run was not due
to any merit the opera possessed; it was probably
no better or worse than other works of the same
composer which all met with so little appreciation
from the public that Desormery gave up music

* MM. E. and J. de Goncourt call the opera, in one place *Euthyme
et Lyris* (p. 98, ed. 1893) and a little later *Euthyme et Licoris* (p. 122)

and became a school-master. Late in life he again
produced one or two operas, which he had touched
and retouched during his period of pedagogy, and
they failed as completely as the former ones had done.

The fact was that the ever-diminishing partisans
of the French school regarded *Euthyme* as their
"last ditch." The poor little opera was the swan-
song of an expiring style, and Sophie Arnould was
the last great singer of the old school. For these
reasons therefore they crowded the Opera House
whenever *Euthyme* was given, and applauded music
and artistes.

The Gluckists, on the other hand, also came in
members. The opera they considered beneath their
contempt, but the singer they hissed and hooted to
their hearts' content.

Sophie treated these exhibitions of public taste—
or the want of it—with supreme disdain and
indifference, and outwardly betrayed no sign of the
rage these insults must have caused her. Inwardly,
she, no doubt, wished a plague on both their houses.
Through no fault of her own, she managed within
the course of the next few nights to lose the good
opinion of both sides.

Iphigenia, the opera by Gluck in which she had
obtained her greatest success, was reproduced, and
she sang in it, but no longer with the former effect.
Her voice was worn out, and the hissing was loud
and long whenever she began an air.

Unfortunately she enlisted on her side an ally
who was calculated to do her more harm than
good. Queen Marie Antoinette heard how Sophie
Arnould was being treated, and resolved to come
to the singer's assistance. She attended the Opera
two or three nights, and, as long as she was there,
the hissers were silent. But the first night the Queen
was absent, the hissing broke out with redoubled
violence, rather intensified than otherwise by the
Queen's marked partisanship. To the English reader,
who has been educated by poets, painters, and
historians, to regard Marie Antoinette as a beautiful
martyr, little short of being a saint, it may appear
treason to state that she was cold and unsympathetic.
Almost from the first day she arrived in France,
she contrived to run counter to all French feelings
and prejudices, and she was consequently disliked
by all classes. Pride, and the impetuous candour
of youth, had much to do with the original creation
of this feeling, which she was prevented from living
down by the ever-growing admiration for liberty and
contempt for tyrants which began to be felt in France
nearly twenty years before the Revolution.

That Gluck's music did not sooner win its way to
general favour was, perhaps, due to the fact that
the Queen had espoused the cause of the German
musician, and, on the other hand, many of those
who went to the opera to hoot at *Iphigenia* or *Alcestis*
perhaps cared less for French music than for the

pleasure of opposing the Court—meaning more especially the Queen.

Marie Antoinette was therefore the worst possible supporter poor Sophie Arnould could have found. The pent-up wrath of Gluckists and anti-Gluckists fell upon the actress with redoubled vehemence. One of the most unpleasant traits in the character of the " Latin races" is forgetfulness of past services. It is less marked, perhaps, in France than in Italy or Spain, but is painfully evident in each country. France calls herself the spoiled child of Europe, and like a spoiled child she throws away her toys as soon as she tires of them. Actors and actresses— the playthings of the public—experience this most cruelly. No veteran is allowed to lag superfluous on the stage, but is pitilessly hissed as soon as the voice shows the first sign of failing, or old age has dimmed the memory, or weakened the muscles. French and Italian actors know this so well that they usually retire from the stage before their powers begin to wane. *

* "I said I knew nothing against the upper classes by personal observation I must recall it I had forgotten. What I saw their bravest and their fairest do last night, the lowest multitude that could be scraped up out of the purlieus of Christendom would blush to do, I think. They assembled by hundreds, and even thousands, in the great Theatre of San Carlo to do—what? Why simply to make fun of an old woman—to deride, to hiss, to jeer at an actress they once worshipped, but whose beauty is faded now, and whose voice has lost its former richness Everybody spoke of the rare sport there was to be. They said the theatre would be crammed because Frezzolini was going to sing It was said she could not sing well now, but then the people liked to see her, anyhow. And so

Sophie Arnould was neither an old, nor an ugly woman, and if her voice had lost somewhat in power or sweetness, that was a trifling set-off against the nineteen years of stage-life during which she had been the idol of all Parisian theatre-goers. It was on one of these occasions that she had to deliver the line,

" *You long for me to be gone,*"

we went And everytime the woman sang they hissed and laughed—the whole magnificent house—and as soon as she left the stage they called her on again with applause Once or twice she was encored five and six times in succession, and received with hisses when she appeared, and discharged with hisses and laughter when she had finished—then instantly encored and insulted again! And how the high-born knaves enjoyed it! White-kidded gentlemen and ladies laughed till the tears came, and clapped their hands in very ecstasy when that unhappy old woman would come meekly out for the sixth time, with uncomplaining patience, to meet a storm of hisses! It was the cruellest exhibition—the most wanton, the most unfeeling The singer would have conquered an audience of American rowdies by her brave, unflinching tranquillity (for she answered encore after encore, and smiled and bowed pleasantly, and sang the best she possibly could, and went bowing off, through all the jeers and hisses, without ever losing countenance or temper), and surely in any other land than Italy her sex and her helplessness must have been an ample protection to her—she could have needed no other. Think what a multitude of small souls were crowded into that theatre last night! If the manager could have filled his theatre with Neapolitan souls alone, without the bodies, he could not have cleared less than ninety millions of dollars. What traits of character must a man have to enable him to help three thousand miscreants to hiss, and jeer, and laugh at one friendless old woman, and shamefully humiliate her? He must have *all* the vile mean traits there are My observation persuades me (I do not like to venture beyond my own personal observation) that the upper classes of Naples possess those traits of character Otherwise they may be very good people, I cannot say "

Mark Twain *The Innocents Abroad*, chap XXIX

Several similar instances have occurred within the present writer's personal experience

and the audience gave a personal application to the
words, and burst into thunders of applause.

Perhaps some doubt may reasonably be felt as
to the truth of this story. It seems to have originated with La Harpe, and was included by him in
one of the letters on dramatic and literary events which
he sent every month to a Russian Grand-Duke.
He was a disagreeable, fault-finding man, and there
are very few plays, books, or persons for whom he
had a good word. He suffered from some skin-
disease, which was most likely psoriasis, or eczema,
which no doubt made him irritable. Many of his
contemporaries call him a leper, and he may have
remembered that Sophie had said of his " classical"
drama that he had inherited nothing from the an-
cients except a " classical" disease. That was not
calculated to make him more favourably inclined
towards the actress, and may perhaps account for
the story.

For it seems difficult to believe that a high-spirited
woman like Sophie Arnould would continue to appear for a year or more, and be hissed every time
she came on the stage, with the exception of those
nights when the Queen was present. If she did,
the only explanation we can give is that she endured
the taunts of the public for the sake of the five
louis she received for every performance, and, even
admitting that hypothesis, would the managers have
continued to pay a sum which, as we have seen,

some of her rivals deemed to be excessive, to a
singer who no longer attracted good houses?

Moreover, though she was in pecuniary difficulties,
she was not yet reduced to such straits that the
money she earned was a necessity to her. She had
still a house, and a notary who paid her 50 louis
a month out of the rents and other monies she was
supposed to lodge in his hands—but which she
sometimes omitted to do.

Some of the letters which M. Gauthier-Villars
recently discovered, refer to this period and show
that Sophie was beginning to feel the everlasting
want of pence, and was compounding with some
of her creditors, and sending others to the unfortunate notary, Alleaume. There is a characteristic
touch in the following letters, in which it will be
noticed that those creditors who agreed to accept
half, or less, of the amount due to them are called
" Monsieur", but those who wanted the whole amount
of their bill are only denominated " Sieur."

"Bonjour, good little Alleaume,—how are you?
Why have you been so long without coming to see
me?—it is very unkind of you. You ought to be
very sure that I have not yet received the thousand
crowns about which I spoke, since I have not
handed you that sum, for I am a man of honour
and I should have brought it or sent it if I had
received it. Payment has been put off till Tuesday,
for it is a bill at ten days and is not due till that

date. Really you ought to be angry with me for having sent my creditors to you without giving you the money to pay them. There is a certain saddler in the world, for instance, named M. Fromond, to whom I owe 750 livres which I ought to pay in full, but who will be satisfied with half the amount of his debt, and there is Sieur Billionard, glazier, who wants 200 francs to settle his old account. There is M. Fropier, wine merchant, who must certainly have 600 livres, for I owe him four times as much or nearly so. I have a tailor continually working for my servants, who also should have a reasonable amount in account, and a good woman who supplies wood, to whom I owe 620 livres for last winter without counting the supply for this year; and there is a butcher, etc., etc. When I think of all these, I tremble in anticipation. On my word, my friend, if you and Morin—who is willing to advance me some funds—do not have pity on me, I must die in the hospital, though I have no great liking for that establishment. All that I can promise you is not to commit any extravagance, and to send you all the money I can get. I can't say fairer than that. The best thing is, that I swear solemnly to keep my promise. Adieu, my good Alleaume, I wish you good health."

And the letter winds up with protests of affection in which the familiar "tu" is employed three or four times. The epistle is dated October 11, 1776.

Perhaps the notary was touched by this sign of affectionate familiarity, for he paid the bills as desired, and it is to be hoped received the thousand crowns on the following Tuesday.

In November there is another short note addressed to the notary to tell him that the doctor had ordered her to retire to her hermitage for change of air, and she longs for the pleasure of embracing her dear friend, who for the last month had treated her as though she had been plague-stricken.

Hardly a fortnight later, she is writing to tell her good friend many things, and firstly that she is out of funds. Three weeks afterwards she was in funds, and sends the notary 3000 francs out of 4200 she had received. She hopes he will not take it in bad part that she has kept back fifty louis, for the month on which they are about to enter (January) is a very expensive one, and, though she hates the custom, she is obliged to conform to it. She asks the notary to send her back certain "big green books" in order that she may see how much she owes her creditors, and she will send him a full and complete account of all her debts, in order that he might rid her of that cursed race—her creditors—as soon as he possibly could. The letter concludes with a renewal of all the promises she has made to be more economical in the future, and she hopes that he will be "edified" when he comes to see her, by the order which prevails in her house from the cellar to the garret.

Whether the notary ever went, and whether he was greatly impressed by the order he found, we know not, but it is certain that the poor man could do little to decrease the ever swelling army of creditors who continued to worry the unfortunate actress until the end of her days.

CHAPTER XI.

Papa Alleaume—A visit from Voltaire—Mesmer and the lap-dog—A thirteen year old wife—Alexandrine's marriage—Mlle Laguerre—A little house at Clichy—Forgiving a thief—Sophie and the Revolutionary Committee—"Paraclete Sophie"

(1777—1792)

WE have now reached the beginning of the long downhill career of poor Sophie Arnould. A year or two of effort to keep her reputation as an *artiste*, when that failed, an endeavour to maintain her place amongst the fast women, and then, as voice failed and lovers slipped away, the gradual transition from riches to poverty—poverty to penury—penury to starvation, and finally the unknown grave in the Montmartre Cemetery. The story is a sad one— not more sad perhaps than thousands of others— but there is an added pathos when the victim has been beautiful, talented, and witty.

At any rate the task of describing the downfall of the great actress will not be a long one. As she dropped down rung after rung of the social ladder, she fell out of the memory of men; the newspapers no longer teemed with accounts of her dramatic successes or failures; if her wit was as bright as ever, none cared to record it.

If she could have foreseen to what misery she would have been reduced, she would perhaps have entrusted Papa Alleaume with some part of her savings, but she could not be other than extravagant, even when she knew that one of the best sources of her wealth—her voice—had failed. If she ever cherished any hopes that something of its pristine vigour would return, every fresh occasion on which she appeared at the Opera must have served to further dissipate the delusion.

In March, 1777, she was again singing her old part of Iphigenia, but she had lost her power of holding the audience spell-bound, and was relentlessly hissed. The Queen again tried to stem the tide of popular opinion, by attending the theatre and loudly applauding the actress, but her intervention "did not prevent the malcontents from continuing their indecent manœuvres."*

Yet she must still have had some admirers. Hardly a fortnight later she attended the sale of the property of M. Randon de Boisset. A bust of Mlle Clairon was put up, and a bid was made for it. Sophie Arnould promptly doubled the amount, and acquired the statue of the great actress. This tempted someone in the room to write a wretchedly bad epigram in which he said that no one had a

---

Bachaumont. March 7th, 1777.

better right to the portrait of Melpomene than the
sister of Apollo.

She seems to have been fond of attending sales,
and at one of them she uttered what is perhaps the
neatest sarcasm recorded of her. Owing to the
reckless extravagance of Mlle Laguerre, and the rapid
manner in which she ruined her rich lovers, her
furniture and effects were frequently being sold. At
one of these sales, a Court lady whose morals were
no better than those of the actress, complained bitterly of the very high prices fetched by the luxurious
furniture of the *demi-mondaine.* " Yet you would not
mind giving cost price I suppose," said Sophie quietly.

Yet only four or five days after purchasing this
bust, Sophie was writing another begging letter to
her notary.

"Sunday, March 24th, 1777.

" Well, *petit père* Alleaume, I never see you now,
and I ask myself why?—why this indifference to
poor Sophie?—for it is not kind of you at all to
avoid people who love you. You will reply to
that, 'but it is you who never see me unless you
have something to ask.'

"Wait and see if I never ask for anything unless
I visit you. Here for example. *Will you please
advance me my month's allowance?* for I am quite
without funds

"Will *petit papa* Alleaume remain inflexible for
four days to the request of Sophie?"

13

Perhaps she got the fifty louis which papa Alleaume was to allow her each month; apparently she did, for the notary appears to have been left in peace for the next six weeks—unless one or two of the little wheedling, coaxing, begging letters have been lost. But in May there comes a long wail of distress, though the actress tries to assume, with not much success, an affectation of gaiety. Every gun in the feminine battery is brought to bear on the notary, with a view to render him less obdurate.

"Tuesday, May 14th, 1777.

"You are wrong to grumble at me, my dear Alleaume, for no one gives more time and attention to their affairs than I do, since the good advice you gave me, and especially since I reflected how cruel it was of me to worry my friends and to suffer their reproaches, just or unjust. For example you, my dear Alleaume, make my position terrible, because you condemn me unjustly. I have passed your door twice, and your young gentlemen can tell you so, for one of them took the trouble to come to my carriage door and talk to me. I went, my friend, *primo*, to see you, because I love you above all, and *segondo* (*sic*) to tell you why you have received neither the rent nor the five hundred livres, and I expected also to get an advance on the last 1200 livres that you have refused *innumainement* (*sic*) to pay me just at a time when it was most needful.

" Oh, it is wrong of you. You see then, my dear sir, from these facts, that you have most unjustly plagued me and grumbled at me; in fact it is I who ought to grumble in my turn, because you never sent me any money at the end of the month as arranged, and I must die of hunger, and bother my head to know how to do a lot of things with no money. I have made out a statement of my debts and receipts that is a work worthy of the Romans;—Sully, that great man, never did anything better, or more clearly showed the condition of France. You give me 50 louis a month for my household expenses and keep. Good! that is all right when you give me the sum in cash, but when you leave me a sum to receive and I don't get it, like the 1000 francs from the King, what do you expect me to do with the 200 francs that you give me? Am I to dig for my living all the rest of the month? I comfort myself with the thought that I cheated you out of a sum that ought to have gone to pay other things. Oh, I was wrong, but you revenge yourself by stopping next month's allowance. Well, which of us two was right?—you were, my friend. And I was wrong to give you trouble, when you give yourself so much to put my finances in order. I swear to you, though you may be rather incredulous as to the state of my mind, that when you have put my little business clear and straight— I promise you on my word as a living being that

I will think twice before I incur the least expense.
It is not possible for me to become miserly—it is
a disgusting vice; I prefer to be ridiculous enough
to be reasonable, and really become so.

"Here is a long letter, at least for a head like
mine It will prove to you, my friend, that you know
how to make everything pleasant, and that friendship, which is a very good thing, can improve all
things, even the most disagreeable, such as business,
and mine above all. Still if I could only do yours
for you, well and good—but—I can see you laughing
at that phrase, and hear you say to yourself: 'By
God, that woman will soon drive me to the hospital!'—
but it is not there that I want to see you, but a
little farther off, at Port à Langlois in the hovel of
your Sophie, who is going to settle there next
Saturday.

"Good-bye, my friend, come and see me and let
me kiss you as much as I love you."

As the year goes on Sophie's affairs—in spite of
her re-iterated promises of reform—become worse
and worse, though towards the end of this same
month (May) she sends her notary 1200 francs, which
would have been more but that she has been lending
money to some honest people who were in distress.
She wants to raise money by a mortgage on her
country house, whilst her old lover, Belanger, is
arranging terms with Prince d'Hénin, and she hopes

M. Alleaume will help him, because the architect is "a good and honest creature." That is more than she can say for the people with whom she is settling the mortgage business; they "think of nothing but crowns and crowns."

An undated letter which perhaps was written towards the close of the year, but which M. Henry Gauthier-Villars seems to think was written about this period, shows that Sophie is as improvident as ever, though she still chatters airily about retrenchment, and boasts that she will commit hardly any(!) foolish extravagances. The notary probably read that as signifying not more than usual. The letter is a good specimen of her nervous, agitated style.

"Ah, good-day, my good friend: it is an age since I saw you or embraced you; when are you going to spend a morning with me? Do you know that I have learned a good lot of sense since the beginning of this year? Do you know that I mean to keep my word and commit hardly any foolish extravagances and you will see that you will be very well satisfied with poor Sophie. A propos of business, have you heard anything of the three thousand six hundred livres that my brother, the *procureur*, ought to have repaid me last October? It seems to me that the gentleman does not hurry himself much.

"If you knew how many small debts I have paid off you would be well satisfied with your Sophie. I have not yet got into my den, but as soon as I have, I should like to meet you and talk over all this business at our ease. If, *en attendant*, you would like to come this evening and eat a truffled turkey, much bigger and a thousand times more of a *dinde* than I am, you will be welcome."

And the letter ends with some remarks about her sons, who were seemingly at school, and who each ask for a tip of twelve francs—which does not seem excessive.

On the 17th June there is a short note with quite a Mantalini touch about it to complain that an execution, or something of the kind, has been put in for the beggarly little account of 196 francs.

The frequent promises of amendment now made little impression on the notary. He remained obdurate to all her appeals, closed his strong-box with a snap, and refused to see Sophie or send her any money, though she might charm ever so sweetly; in fact he was rather huffed—apparently because she had broken the agreement between them, and, not content with her allowance, had appropriated some of the money she had received during the month of July instead of passing it over to him.

And so the months roll on, resembling each other only too closely. The doors of the Royal Academy of Music were virtually closed against her, and her name no longer figures at the head of the list of *artistes* but appears half way down as a singer of "ordinary parts," and even those she either never got the chance of performing, or else refused. But she still occupied some place in society and was looked up to—by men at least—on account of her wit.

In February, 1778, the Marquis de Villette, who had married the adopted daughter of Voltaire, presented his wife, and asked Sophie what she thought of her.

"She is a very nice edition of the *Pucelle,*" replied the actress.

Voltaire was induced to pay a visit to Sophie Arnould. He regarded himself as little short of a King and had duly notified her of his intention to call at a certain hour on a certain day.

Sophie was a clever woman, in everything except money affairs, and she knew what sort of reception would please the old man. She collected a band of the children of her relatives, headed by her own daughter, who was then just eleven years of age, and as Voltaire entered the apartment, they all sprang forward, and hugged, and kissed him. The philosopher was highly pleased. "You all want to kiss me, and I have no face left," he said laughingly.

He talked to Sophie for a long time, and it is a pity there was no reporter present to record the conversation, which could not have failed to be witty. Only one scrap has reached us.

"Ah, Madame," said the aged poet, "I am now eighty-four years of age, and I have committed eighty-four foolish acts in the course of my life."

"That is a mere nothing," replied the actress with charming candour, "I am not yet forty, and I have committed more than a thousand."

Many lesser celebrities were also to be found in the salons of Sophie Arnould, for now that she had practically left the stage, she tried to pose as a sort of modern Aspasia. Even Jean Jacques was sometimes to be seen seated at her table, D'Alembert, Duclos, Diderot, Beaumarchais, Favart, Dorat ("as hard, as cold, and as handsome as a marble statue," Sophie said of him), Marmontel, Bernard, and a host of lesser luminaries were frequent visitors. The Prince de Ligne, ever on the look out for "copy," where it could be obtained without loss of dignity, also came occasionally. No man of wit *and* position he asserted, should ever be found at the "suppers of the impure," but he made exceptions in favour of Sophie Arnould and Julie, who afterwards married Talma, the celebrated actor—a condescension for which it is to be hoped those two *impures* were properly thankful.

With the leaders of the *demi-monde*, Sophie Arnould was hardly likely to be a favourite. She had not the money to vie with them in extravagant entertainments, and her biting wit estranged those who would still have been on friendly terms with her. One of them, Mlle Dubois, a very indifferent actress, who had managed to get herself accepted at the Comédie Française, was notorious for her numerous love affairs, and for her parsimony. She made so much and she spent so little of the large sums she received from her lovers, that when she died she left property which brought in an income of 25.000 francs a year. She was of about the same age as Sophie Arnould, or perhaps even a little older. At all events she complained in Sophie's presence that "it was quite terrible to think she was so near her fortieth birthday."

"Take courage, my dear," replied Sophie in her usual spiteful manner, "and be consoled with the reflection that every day takes you farther away from it."

Certainly no one could bring a charge of parsimony against poor Sophie Arnould. This year, Mesmer visited Paris, and professed to cure all diseases by means of animal magnetism. Everyone who had, or could pretend to, any complaint, went to be healed, and large sums were pocketed by the arch-swindler.

Either Sophie was not suffering from any particular malady at that time, or she had sense enough to keep out of Mesmer's hands, and when some of her fashionable friends begged her to go and see the illustrious doctor, she replied that she did not need his professional services, but that if he could cure her lap-dog, which had been ailing for some time past, she would believe in him.

Mesmer does not seem to have been offended at the proposal—perhaps he was anxious to prove that his system was not dependent on the credulity or blind faith of the patient, as many people asserted. At all events the dog was sent, and was returned a few days later, apparently well. Mesmer sent a request that Sophie would give him a testimonial to say that the animal was cured. Sophie complied, and Mesmer hastened to show the letter to his followers, and even published it in the papers.

In this he was a little too premature. Three or four days later the dog died, much to the delight of the wits, who twitted Mesmer with his failure, and asked Sophie what could have induced her to give such a certificate.

"I have nothing to reproach myself with," she replied, "the poor animal died in excellent health."

In the August of this year Sophie Arnould and Madame Larrivée were commanded to sing at a concert given by the Duc de Chartres. Sophie's voice failed her, and she was loudly hissed. A few nights later, the Duc and Duchesse were walking in the garden, and passed under the windows of Sophie's house. She saw them, threw open the window, and began to sing, and, as her voice was in good condition that night, she was loudly applauded by her royal visitors, and others who had collected to hear her.

It seems evident from this anecdote, which is related by Bachaumont, that Sophie was still occupying the same apartment on the north side of the Palais Royal.

There are few other references to Sophie in the years which preceded the Revolution. We might quote many of her letters to the notary Alleaume, but they are all alike. They profess to be written in high spirits, but the fun is too evidently forced. We can see the tear marks through the grin, and we know as well what is coming at the end of each letter as Alleaume and his clerks did—an earnest demand for the next month's money.

Her spirit was broken by the worry of money troubles.

She was no longer on the books of the Opera except as a pensioner, but she often attended the performances and sat in the green-room. Her wit and common-sense made her much looked up to, and her opinion was asked in all theatrical matters. The affairs of the Opera were still in a muddle, and occasional little disturbances took place. A magistrate, a certain M. Amelot, proposed rather stringent measures. He had formerly been President of the Parliament of Burgundy, and as Parliaments even some years before the Revolution had become difficult to manage, he had not been very successful. He explained his scheme for restoring order in the affairs of the Opera-house to several listeners, of whom Sophie Arnould was one. "You must understand," she said, "that it is more difficult to manage an Opera company than it is a Parliament."

In 1779 she succeeded in selling her house at Port l'Anglois for 20.000 francs, though she had expected to get 30.000 frs. for it. She announces the sale to Alleaume in a characteristic note.

"At last, my friend, our house is sold—I say ours because the interest you take in my affairs, and the friendship I have for you make me regard all our property as common. I look to you, my dear Alleaume, to make all the arrangements necessary in this matter: I have sold the house for twenty thousand francs without the furniture. Circumstances—the war for one thing, and the general want of money for another, have made me decide to sell. What do you think about it? I should perhaps have had to wait till the spring, and then perhaps I should have had a better offer, but, who knows? things might be better or they might be worse, so I said to myself, as any sensible woman would, 'A bird in the hand is worth two in the bush.' Adieu, my friend, see to all this business, for I don't want to meddle with it except to sign anything you want me to sign."

Very soon afterwards she complains that she is laid up with a cold 'as big as the towers of Notre Dame,' but as soon as she gets well she will call upon him, "and kiss him three times on the eye, and settle up accounts with him."

Old Alleaume must have had a shrewd suspicion that she would find the second part of the promise much more difficult than the first.

A little later she announces to him that she has 2000 crowns to hand over to him—or rather had, for to spare him the trouble of settling with all her small creditors she has been paying them herself and will hand over the receipts to him. She confesses herself ashamed of all the trouble she has given him, and thanks him for the "noble and disinterested manner he has behaved to her." She then invites him to dinner on the following Tuesday, when he will find at her house some persons who will be glad to talk over her affairs with him—probably persons from whom she was trying to borrow money.

Towards the close of this year (September, 1779) Sophie took a friend to board with her. This was Mlle Raucourt, a very pretty and very clever young actress of whom mention has previously been made, and whose chastity for a time withstood all the temptations of the libertines of the Court

At last she fell from the paths of virtue, and as is not unusual in such cases went to the other extreme. In fact she became so vicious and depraved that the actors of the Comédie Française refused to associate with her, which gives one the idea that she must have been very bad indeed. By some means or other, however, she managed to enlist the virtuous Marie Antoinette on her side, and the Queen ordered that she should be re-instated in the company, notwithstanding the protest of the actors and actresses, who declared that her misconduct and libertinage rendered her unworthy to associate with the members of the Théâtre Français. She therefore returned in triumph, and Sophie Arnould received her with open arms.

The two became close friends and when Mlle

Raucourt made her re-appearance on the boards in the character of Dido, Sophie packed the house with her friends, and insured a favourable reception for her *protégée*.

Bachaumont, who glories in any scandalous tale, declares that some three or four months later—in the beginning of January, 1780—Mlle Raucourt ran away from the house in company with Sophie's protector the Prince d'Hénin, and that Sophie was so enraged at this base ingratitude that she vowed to take a terrible vengeance on the pair, and would surely have done so if they had not taken refuge at Bagatelle, the residence of Comte d'Artois.

We rather fancy though the story is not true, and that Prince d'Hénin had ceased to be the protector of Sophie Arnould long before the younger actress came to her house. Nor is it very probable that such an intrigue could have been carried on without the quick-witted Sophie observing it. If it had been managed without her knowledge she would not have been likely, we think, to threaten personal injury to the offenders. She would far more likely have revenged herself by some bitter epigram. On the whole we are inclined to think that the story was invented and sent to Bachaumont by one of the actors of the Comédie Française, in the hope that it would reach the ears of the Queen, and open her eyes as to the real character of the person to whom she had extended her royal protection.

One of the supposed adorers still faithful to the declining star was a certain M. Murville. He wrote epigrams, which are so bad that they are not worth translating, about Sophie, and was supposed to be one of her lovers, but he suddenly declared his passion for Alexandrine, Sophie's daughter, and proposed for her hand.

Alexandrine was at this time barely more than thirteen years of age—a gawky, red-headed child, who, in spite of her appearance, was not without a good share of her mother's wit.

She was, moreover, exceedingly precocious, and possibly not as innocent as girls of thirteen usually are. Her features were not pretty, but her wealth of reddish golden hair made her look passable. Dr. Millen, who annotated the copy of "Arnoldiana" which afterwards fell into the hands of Messrs. de Goncourt, declares that before she was married she had been the mistress of the Comte d'Artois and "my lord" Stuart, but that seems hardly credible, though considering that she had perhaps hardly ever seen her father, and her mother was cynically indifferent to all questions of morality, she could hardly be expected to be a paragon of virtue. The few anecdotes that are recorded of her have no pleasant sound. She seems to have had a perfect knowledge of her mother's habits of life, and to have alluded to them pretty freely and sarcastically, nor does Sophie Arnould appear to have been at all a good mother.

At the best, Alexandrine was a conceited and very fast child, and perhaps she was far worse. She had lived in bad society, and if Sophie ever said, as the anecdotes record, that the old *roués* who came to her house came "to look for the Golden Fleece"— alluding to her daughter's hair—we may get an insight into what Alexandrine's character was likely to have been. On the other hand it is possible that the anecdotes related of her may not have been true. Bachaumont and his followers had no good word to say for anyone, and knowing the mother was out of favour with the public they were not likely to spare the daughter.

At any rate the poor child suffered for her mother's vices. Sophie allowed her to be married, at a time when she ought to have been at school, to a young man who perhaps never really cared for his child-wife, and who beat and ill-used her during the five years she lived with him.

What induced Sophie to consent to this ill-assorted marriage we know not. Perhaps she felt herself unable to keep the child, for debts became oppressive and creditors more insolent every day. Possibly, like all people who are satirical, she rather dreaded Alexandrine's sharp tongue, or was ashamed of the child knowing how vicious her mother was. One of the anecdotes of Alexandrine records that she said, "I shall soon be as old as my mother, for I get a year older each year, and she gets a year younger."

The joke is certainly much older than the Eighteenth Century.

Murville * was a young man, and a very indifferent poet. He had perpetrated a few epigrams about Sophie, which though meant to be complimentary were atrociously bad. The actress said of him that he was a bore who looked like a stage footman, but Alexandrine seems to have fallen in love with him, and easily obtained her mother's consent.

The marriage took place in November, 1780, at the Church of St. Roch. Murville who was exactly twice the age of his wife was connected with several *bourgeois* families, and all these worthy citizens and their wives were present at the ceremony. When the bride's mother was introduced to all these couples, she said with the cynical effrontery which characterised her, "It appears that I am the only unmarried woman present."

Dr. Millin, who says he was present at the wedding breakfast, records that a certain Chevalier Dolomieu was there, who passed for being Alexandrine's lover. Eye-glasses were then made Y-shaped, and the Chevalier had a pair of these glasses which he showed to the guests. De Murville tried them, and declared they suited his sight exactly. Sophie noticed that they resembled a pair of horns.

"You had better keep them," she said, "as a wedding present from Dolomieu."

---

* He seems to have had not the slightest right to the *de* which he usually prefixed to his name

Alexandrine was not, perhaps, a very sympathetic companion, but Sophie's life must have been duller without her. In a very few weeks Alexandrine came with streaming eyes to complain of her husband's cruelty. Sophie remonstrated with Murville, but she was now his mother-in-law and the complimentary epigrams he used to shower upon her changed to insults.

Misfortunes crowded upon the "poor fairy" as she was called. Her house was beset with creditors clamouring for their money, and the notary remained deaf to all appeals for monetary assistance. Her lovers had deserted her, female friends betrayed and deceived her, the marriage of her daughter had proved unhappy; and finally if the unfortunate actress showed herself in public she was pursued by cowardly brutes who but a few years before had been ready to worship her, but who now hooted and howled in chorus a line from one of the operas in which she used to sing.

"Charon calls, do you hear his voice?"

Sophie Arnould was not a good woman, and perhaps deserved all the wrongs and insults she received, but all the same one cannot help feeling that if half a dozen able-bodied men had been provided with good long whips and told to go amongst that crowd and lay about them it would not have been a bad thing.

Sophie's only amusement was to visit the Opera, for though she was no longer a singer she still had the right of entry, and her advice on theatrical matters was always practical and sensible, though not always appreciated by the persons to whom it was given. Her misfortunes had somewhat soured her temper, and her wit, which was never of a kindly nature, became more caustic than ever Many of her sallies, however, are unsuited for publication, being far too outspoken for modern ears.

One of the few satisfactions she had was that her old enemy Rosalie Levasseur was no longer playing the chief parts. They were entrusted to Mlle Laguerre who was quite as immoral as any of her predecessors, and in addition was fond of the bottle. On the second night of *Iphigenia in Tauris* (January 1781) she was so intoxicated that she could hardly perform two acts. A country gentleman who was seated next to Sophie Arnould, who was in the front of the house, asked whether the Opera was Iphigenia in Aulis, or Iphigenia in Tauris?

"Neither," replied Sophie; "it is Iphigenia in Champagne."

At the conclusion of the performance Mlle Laguerre was arrested and sent to prison, where she remained thirteen days, which caused her to register a vow that she would never in future take more than thirteen glasses of champagne at a sitting. It was perhaps as well that the term of imprisonment was not further prolonged.

She was as extravagant as most of her sisterhood,

and had ruined a score of lovers. One night she told the manager that God would never pardon her because she had ruined a Bishop. He replied that he had heard she had driven a good many other people into bankruptcy, amongst them being a well-known banker.

"Oh," she replied, "that was the best action I ever did."

As might be expected, Mlle Laguerre was a woman after Sophie's own heart, and the elder actress hardly ever said anything sarcastic about the younger; but others felt the force of her tongue. Mlle Duplant, another actress, had a natural son to whom she was greatly attached. She had made over to him, whilst quite a child, a small estate she possessed, and she expressed her intention of having him educated "in the bosom of his family."

"In that case," said Sophie slyly, "you must send him to the College of the Four Nations"—a remark which Mlle Duplant did not like.

The visits to the Opera had to cease, for the house was destroyed by fire June 8th, 1781. From that time mentions of Sophie get rarer and rarer. In 1782 she undertook to train a pupil for the stage, a certain Mlle Aurora, but it is probable that Sophie's only intention in so doing was to spite Mlle Raucourt, who, the scandal-mongers asserted, had refused to accept a pupil who was better looking and cleverer than herself

For the next few years we hear nothing of Sophie
Arnould. Like many other female rakes she took
to devotion, or rather tried to and failed, for directors
of conscience, she said were worse than directors
of the Opera. By the bankruptcy of the Prince de
Guémené, in 1782, she lost some 30.000 francs, though
we do not exactly know how, and it was probably
this which induced her to quit Paris. She took a
small house at Clichy-la-Garenne, just outside Paris,
and there she lived quietly, except that she seems to
have kept open house for all her friends.

In 1785 she was joined there by her daughter,
who was unable any longer to tolerate the ill usage
of her husband, and had sued for a divorce on the
ground of cruelty.

Alexandrine declares in the affidavit that she made
before Commissaire Chenu that "since she had the
misfortune to marry Murville she had never known
an instant's peace. He had often struck her, as many
witnesses could testify. He had turned her out of
doors at one o'clock in the morning only a few days
after the birth of her first child." A few months later
we find her petitioning the Minister to permit her
to become a chorus singer at the Opera, but her
request was not granted apparently.

Alexandrine at last managed to get a divorce
from her husband. She was then only nineteen—
an age at which most girls are not married.

Murville threatened to be revenged on his mother-in-law for giving shelter to his wife He circulated a report that he was about to produce at the Théâtre Français a play in which the principal characters would be Sophie Arnould, her old lover Belanger, and the actor Florence who was believed to have also been one of Sophie's most favoured lovers. The play was never produced—probably Murville had not the brains to write it himself, or the money to pay anyone to do it for him.

During the years that she lived at Clichy we hear very little of Sophie. She had plenty of company if Millin is to be believed. He relates:

" I sometimes went to see Mlle Arnould at Clichy. One day I found a large assemblage. There were twenty persons at table. I was about to leave. She called me back, saying, 'Come in! The son of my cook has married the daughter of my gardener. Both the families and all my servants are my guests. We celebrate the pleasures of Love and Equality.'

" In the evening both her sons came. They wanted money and she had none to give them. 'Well,' she said, 'there are two horses in the stable; take one each.' And they went away with the two horses."

The anecdote sounds genuine, it is so very characteristic.

Another visitor records that when he called upon her she invited him to stop to dinner, and promised that if he did she would prepare a *roux de veau* for him.

"What, can you make a *roux de veau?*" he asked.

"Why; did you think that I could only make a *rousse?*" replied Sophie laughing, and pointing to Alexandrine.

Money troubles, however, still pressed heavily on Sophie. On the last day of the year 1788 we find her writing to Boutin, a rich man whom she had known in her prosperous days. She begs him to read the letter, and call to mind the delicacy of her behaviour towards the illustrious ingrates to whom she had given her heart, happiness, and the pleasures of youth. She pardons these ingrates for having forgotten her attractions and her care,—but will not pardon them for having forgotten her tenderness. There is a touch of pathos in the remark that after twenty years of glory, flattery, and ease, she has only herself to rely on. She goes on to say that owing to the expense of bringing up her children, who are great lords in the morning, and very little shop-keepers at night, and of starting them in the world, she is nearly ruined.

She still has some 20 or 25 thousand francs a year, but she owes at least one year's income. She therefore proposes to borrow 24.000, which she will pay back in four years at the rate of 6000 francs per year. But "as we all are mortal," she proposes to give a mortgage on her house at Clichy—"which although it will not fetch what I gave for it, is worth a thousand louis"—and also all the furniture in her house in the Rue Caumartin. She winds up by asking Boutin to procure this loan for her from friend Brichart, who was probably a money-lender; and she swears she will keep her promise to pay with "certainty, honour, and probity."

When she next writes to Boutin (13 January, 1789) she has seen Brichart, who like most money-lenders, has not the sum available, for at least a month, and she therefore asks Boutin to advance her 5000 francs till that time.

A little later it is not 5000 francs but 12.000 that she requires. She writes begging letters to all her acquaintances, and when they send her money, or even evince "an intention to oblige her," she overwhelms them with gratitude, and declares that if it is true, as learned men assert, that the soul never perishes, her soul will remember the obligation even after death.

But let us leave the "poor fairy" struggling vainly against her debts. At all events she could feel for the distress of others. On 21st January, a man named Bompas was arrested at the Clichy gate with a lot of clothes, a pair of candlesticks, a silver mustard pot, and other articles, many of which were marked with the monogram "S. A." and which proved to have been stolen from a house in the Rue Royale, Clichy, belonging to the Demoiselle Arnould. Sophie found that Bompas was a journeyman carpenter who had been out of work for six weeks, and that this was his first offence, as far as was known.

Whereupon "with the permission of the magistrates," she declined to prosecute, and Bompas was released.

Whether Sophie took any part in the Revolution we cannot say, but we think it highly improbable. The Comte de Tilly makes out that her salon became a sort of Revolutionary Club, at which men of letters, philosophers, politicians and others, assembled, and a similar statement is found in the *Chronique Scandaleuse*, in which her old enemy Champcenety declares that she received at her house all the scum of the human race; that she sent her two sons to the Jacobins to complete their political education and receive the baptism of patriotism, etc., and he finishes by quoting the coarse jest of the Marquis de Louvois, that if Sophie had a bad breath it was because her heart was on her lips.

As far as we know, Sophie continued to live at Clichy till 1790, when she sold the house and purchased an old priory at Luzarches (Seine et Oise) She had never evinced any particular interest in politics, and crippled as she was with debts, it is hardly likely that she would play such an unprofitable part as keeping open house for all the turbulent spirits of the time. Her eldest son had almost completed his twenty-eighth year when the Bastille fell, and her other son was but three years younger, so they were quite able to form their own opinions! Moreover they did not live with their mother, and cared very little about her we fancy.

If she had taken any important part in the events of the early part of the Revolution, she would, in the later days, either not have been "suspected" at all, or "suspected" very much indeed. In the latter case she would have been arrested and sent to Paris to join her friends and fellow actresses at the Conciergerie.

The only time she was interfered with was when she was living at Luzarches, when she received a domiciliary visit from the local committee. They put the usual question to her and she replied, "She was a good citizen; she thoroughly understood the rights of man, and had always practised them"—a remark which was certainly true in one sense, but the double meaning was lost upon the dull peasants. The Committee men expressed their intention of looking through the rooms to see if they could discover any articles which were at all suspicious.

Sophie possessed a small bust representing herself in the "death-scene" in some tragic opera. The eyes were turned up, the mouth was open and all the signs of death were evident. One of the Committee soon discovered this bust, and declared to his fellows that it was unnecessary to search any farther, Citoyenne Arnould was evidently a good patriot, for she had a bust representing the great and good Marat in his last moments.

Sophie could hardly have felt flattered, but she very wisely held her peace, and the Luzarches patriots

left, with many apologies to Citoyenne Arnould, and
compliments on her patriotism, which, they said,
they had both heard from her neighbours, and proved
for themselves, to be above all suspicion.

The house she bought at Luzarches had been the
priory of a small branch of Penitents of the Third
Order of St. Francis. The monks had either fled,
or been dispossessed, and Sophie bought the property for a "mere song." She called it "Paraclete
Sophie," or perhaps the first part of the name had
been bestowed by the former tenants It is to be
feared she did not derive much "comfort" from it.
She also caused to be carved over the door the
inscription, "*Ite, missa est.*"

In this house she lived until four or five years
before her death when she removed to Paris. Her
daughter lived with her for two or three years, when
finding herself very dull and half starved, she married
the son of the local post-master. Sophie was not
very particular in the matter of morals, but she professed to be very disgusted at a divorced woman
marrying whilst the man who was her husband in
the eyes of heaven was still alive

" Divorce is the sacrament of adultery," she said

CHAPTER XII

For nearly twelve years the poor broken-down actress dragged on a miserable career, almost lonely —for it is doubtful whether Alexandrine, though she lived near, often came to see her,—in terrible poverty, and in ill health.

She still corresponded with Belanger, one of the two men who had ever loved her, or whom she had really loved.

His letters to her are evidently meant to cheer and amuse her, and she writes back in a similar strain, complaining good-humouredly of the troubles which oppress her—though she cannot help dropping the mask occasionally.

She writes to him on 27th February, 1793:

" *To Belanger.*

" From Paraclet Sophie.

" February 27th, 1793.

" Well! my beautiful angel, here is your Sophie returned to her poor little cottage. You will know,

my friend, that you have treated me with great indifference whilst I was in Paris, only seeing me
once! although I went twice to find you.

"I am always like those good dogs which come
back at once and lick the hand of the master who
has beaten them. Oh, I was on the point of weeping
more than once, but I said to myself: Well, what
can you do Sophie? Poor Sophie! You can easily
sulk about his belly, but can you sulk about your
own heart? Alas! I returned sadly to my solitude,
where the consolation of hope brightened my future.
Ah! as. I always sing, I find in thinking of all that
has happened to me, that the air and the words of
poor Jacques,

'When I was near thee, etc., etc.,'

marvellously suited my situation, and it is now
the only air which I permit myself....Ah! poor
baby....you will remember it: All my days were
happy! Who will give me back these propitious
days?

"Well, baby, although I no longer count upon
your head, or upon....

"I warn you that I count, and shall count etern-
ally, upon your heart:—Consequently I beg you to
give at this moment a sincere proof of interest and
friendship for your Sophie, in busying yourself a
little in her small affairs: First, about my house of
Clichy-la-Garenne, sold, with right of redemption, to
Citizen Germain, banker at Paris, living in the Place

des Victoires, for I do not know his last name. I
sold it to him for 34 000 francs for three years, but
at the end of two, if I can re-sell it for more, if I
give him back the sum of 24.000 francs which he
has given me, I take possession of it as it stands;
I want 40.000 francs for it, including the looking-
glasses, wainscottings, and all the ornaments. You
know, my friend, that this house cost me more than
65.000 francs, counting all that I have had constructed,
and the buildings, etc., that I have added, so that the
persons who take it will absolutely have nothing but
beds and furniture to bring Try, my beloved, to
hasten this sale for me, because it will bring me
some money, of which I am in great need like all
the rest of the world at the present time. This is
one thing; now for the second. As I think of or-
namenting, and beautifying my retreat and increasing
its value, I plant and sow, as much as I can. If
you could get me some trees, first fruit trees, such
as dwarf apple-trees called 'Sans Paradis,' also
other sorts; some pear, and peach-trees, and a great
many small shrubs, for the groves and flower gardens;
oh! you would give me great pleasure. What a
number of things at one time you will say; but! it
is to trouble you less often, that I ask at once for
all that I want or wish for; I have excellent ground,
and a charming site, as if it were the garden of
Eden. This is why I begin my request by apples,
not that I have an Adam to tempt, or that I am

likely to find a Paris to give me one, but one is
happy to be able all one's life to keep a 'pear against
thirst.' Ah! baby, I venture to make all these demands,
well knowing that you will do all you can for me,
but you are at liberty to refuse my requests, but not
all, for you have only to show your good will in
the affair of the house at Clichy, and if that happens,
then I shall be able to get all I want. Good-bye,
my good baby, my old and unchangeable friend,
never forget that there exists in a corner of this
earth a being who has loved you very tenderly—
with reason and with distraction—and who will love
you to the last sigh of her last moment. And that
being is your Sophie!

"P.S. Let me have news of you, write to me
often at my Paraclet, you know that the first of the
Heloises only wished for the letters of her Abelard
to charm her melancholy, it was she who said to her
lover that the art of writing was invented by the
unhappy and captive lover, etc., etc. Well, once
more good-bye, though the word costs me my heart.

"If love leaves some moments for friendship, give
them to your poor friend."

No doubt Belanger sent her the fruit-trees she
required, and some good advice about her house, but
most of the letters have been lost. There is one
from him dated 16 January, 1795. He had not had
a particularly pleasant time during the worst days

of the Revolution; he had been imprisoned, and had nearly been one of the victims of Thermidor. He recounts his adventures amusingly. As he truly says, many things had happened since they last met, and he feels like the sick man who said to his doctor, " I have had an emetic, and the sacrament, and opium, and extreme unction all in one day; they have treated me like a horse."

Belanger complains that he has been ruined, robbed, imprisoned and married—he was married in prison to Mlle Dervieux, who had been a notorious courtesan—and that when he escaped the executioner, he found that a faithless servant had stolen most of his effects, and the officers of justice had turned upside down and broken what furniture remained, in their search for jewels and money—two kinds of property he had never possessed. When he thought of applying to his friends for help, he found that two thirds of them had had their heads cut off, and the others were afraid of befriending a man who had been in prison.

The poor architect thought that he should at least have a little time to himself now he was at liberty, but the Comité de Sûreté having heard that when he was in prison he had delivered a lecture on the jail experiences of Howard, the philanthropist, jumped to the conclusion that he was a philanthropist himself, and appointed him a kind of " relieving officer." He did not dare to refuse the post, but he grumbles in this letter that " he has to distribute fresh pork,

candles, meat, oil, bread, wood, etc., to the poor, with
the job of looking after all the funerals thrown in, and
all that for a crown (3 francs) a day, for working
from seven in the morning to eleven at night." It
is small wonder that the poor man wishes that he
could be sent back to prison in order that he might
enjoy a little liberty.

In concluding his letter, he says he does not dare to
write anything about her money affairs, but he hopes
to hear from her about her health, her daughter,
and everything that interests her.

Sophie replied in the following long letter.

" *To Belanger*.

" FROM PARACLET SOPHIE.

" The 3rd Ventose, 3rd year of the French Republic,
one and indivisible (February 21st, 1795).

" At last there is an answer from my bel ange, or
to express myself according to my heart, news of
my friend; so you see me once more happy in my
life. Your letter, my friend, has made me experience
all sorts of sensations, and you need not doubt the
rank in which I place them; after the pain, the pleasure.
How much my beloved has suffered!....They have
ruined my bel ange; they have robbed, incarcerated,
and married you....My friend, I did not, but I came
very near, suffering the same torments, the same
persecution; they have ruined me also, they have made

15

domiciliary visits, they would even have proceeded to
imprison me, if the inhabitants of my commune had not
testified for me, but they said so much good of me,
that the committee respected my person, and only
took my fortune, but of what use is riches, to those
who have need of nothing. After all, as I have so
much to tell you about all that, I will reserve it
until I see you, if I still remember it, for I believe
the pleasure of seeing you would make me forget
all my misfortunes and vicissitudes, etc. However,
we are free, once again, we must hope that this
will be the last, and that we shall have no more
tyrants, or ministers, to contend with. The monster
of Gevaudan has been talked of for a long while,
but I believe that the ferocious animal called Robespierre will be talked of for a still longer time. But
let us try to forget all these horrors: that will be
difficult for my heart, since I have to regret one of
the victims, who was dear to me ... . Your friend, the
unhappy Hénin; I do not know if I shall weep for
him much longer, no, but I promise never to forget him.

"Now let us change the subject; you do not know
where I am, nor how I am. Well! I must give
you the details; first of all my habitation was formerly a monastery (which would have been extremely to the taste of our celebrated Ninon). But
my monastery without monks would not have been
as much to her as to me, such as it is, I am not
in a community celebrated for society, for there is

none here, but I am here in a charming retreat,
which would have become a delight, if I had been
able to finish the work that I had begun, but they
have taken all my money. The friend Cambon has
by his algebraic operations, cut arms and legs so
well, that I have a house which is only a carcass,
and which waits for doors and windows until it shall
please God to send me the means; but, for the present, I am a little like the Son of God, who was
made man, I have not where to lay my head; that
is to say, nevertheless, that I am camping provisionally,
in a sort of hovel that I call my house. I have had
built in the dovecot of my ancient monks, a room
which holds a bedstead, a table, and chair, etc., this
is where I lie. But in return I have a beautiful
park, containing all that it is possible to desire for
ornament or use, a superb kitchen garden, a vine-
yard, which has yielded me this year six hogsheads
of wine, a forest, a wood, an orchard, a pond well
stocked with fish, groves, fresh air, beautiful scenery,
good land; this is the fourth year that I have been
here, and I remain in the greatest solitude—but
well! I have not felt one moment's *ennui* since I came
here. All my surroundings are varied; I began building
at first, and then the contest finished for want of
combatants for the cause. But I have planted, taken
up, sown, and reaped; then I have a poultry yard; my
courtiers are very numerous; cocks, hens, turkeys,
pigs, fowls, and rabbits. I also had pigeons, but

the expense of their food made me give up these last. When I have some ground at liberty for their food, well! I shall keep them again, for they are always a resource, and there is much to be gained from them, especially when they are on the table; there they do not worry you. I have quite forgotten the fashionable world and its customs; you see, my friend, I have lived so long like a savage that I can hardly remember the language of human beings. Oh! if I had not my daughter, who sometimes comes to draw me from my lethargy, I believe that I should have forgotten to speak my language, but with respect to my daughter, she is always a droll creature, always witty, you know, she is divorced from Murville! and has re-married here, a fine handsome young man, the son of the postmaster at Luzarches. In short, it is done, you know that provided she is all right at night, she does not trouble herself much appearances in the daytime. This husband ought to have suited her as little as he did me, but she would have him, and she took him. As regards the husband, well, you can have a good idea of what he is, for there is a young man who has been a designer at your place, who has just married his sister; he is an architect called Lépine, he has made a good marriage in all respects; his wife is the sweetest and best creature in the world, and then she is rather rich, all the more so that all her fortune is invested in land, and land to day fetches an exhorbitant price.

There, for once, this is too long a letter, and nevertheless I have not told you a hundredth part of the
things which I had to tell you, for I have a hundred
thousand things to speak to you about; I have a
hundred questions to ask about your actual position,
about the rest of your misfortunes, your wants, and
what not! Do not expect fine phrases from me, my
heart is stupid at that, but remember well, my friend,
that I am the less unfortunate of the pair. You have
the right to share all I possess; I have not forgotten
former times, nor your good qualities and virtues: it
is quite true that one who has always been a good
son, a good parent, a good friend, will also find
good hearts, and that your Sophie is, has been, and
will be, yours to the last hour!

"The first who has leisure, will go to visit the
other; if I go, it will only be for a thousand things.
A thousand kind regards, a thousand thanks to your
wife, for her obliging offer."

A few months later she sent another letter to
Belanger. Possibly there were others in between,
but they have either not been preserved, or not been
discovered.

"From Paraclet Sophie, year 3, 3rd Floreal
(April 22nd, 1795).

"Well, my bel ange, you think then that you are
to get off answering me. Oh, I do not let my

friends off so cheaply as that. I have written to
you twice, and I wish for two answers. One from
you, and one from your companion. And, since
she has set up to be your nurse, she must fulfil
the duties of her position, she must have the goodness (of which she has a good portion in her heart),
to give me news of you, I must say of her also,
but I know she is so pretty, that I think of her as
it says in the song of Beaumarchais, 'Beautiful,
that is to say good.' On my word, my bel ange,
you are not changed, for what you love is always
the same. But *sans compliments*, let me hear from
you Ask her to write about you, and we shall
all three be happy; as for me, if I am not dead of
hunger after this, I will write to you, and until you
will perhaps be weary. We die of hunger here
because we are surrounded by wretches, for there is
corn here for more than a year, so we are far from
real famine. In short, I have been refused 1.500
francs, for a 'septier' of flour, they have such ill
will, that they refuse even cash; they will absolutely
make me die of hunger and take away all my resources.
Commerce at present is nothing but an unruly
brigandage; those who can act the worst succeed.

"The farmers, the millers, the bakers, and even
the butchers, saving the esteem which I have for
representative Legendre, are all beggarly wretches,
who have no law, and no faith, who hold nothing
sacred, and are Judases by nature.

"Poor Republic! I am moved with anger to see so much villainy. Well! am I not in a temper, like Gilles, I who see no one, and who have never wished to meddle with anything, but plant my cabbages, fry, and eat them, for I have become the Maître Jacques of my house, and God knows what a house! Happily I am not given to gluttony, and as poor Favier said, I am not wholly devoted to asparagus, or I should be badly nourished. However that will pass away; that which is immutable, that time or absence can never change, is the tender and constant heart and friendship of your Sophie.

"Come then! let me hear from you both. Do not make me languish, for very soon, perhaps, I shall depart on the long journey, the eternal departure.

"Give my kind regards to Bougainville, I always love that little scamp at school or college.

"P.S. You promised to send me some seeds; do not forget me, my friends, for I am always planting.

"With respect to planting, I have not told you that a person named Lépine, whom I believe I have seen in a corner of your studio, has married the sister of my latest son-in-law; notice well that I do not say the last.... because Mrs. Alexandrine may order it otherwise.... he is nevertheless rather a good fellow....

"I embrace your wife; if this kiss should seem to be too unsubstantial, let her give it to you, and you can give her another."

As the years rolled on Sophie became poorer
and poorer. She had no skill in farming, and what
her estate did produce was sold to the peasants for
less than it had cost to grow. She no longer pesters
her friends or her notary about her property, for
she has nothing but the mis-named Paraclete—af
ruin with only one small habitable room, all the
other apartments being without doors and windows

In January, 1797, she came to Paris to try to get
some of the arrears of her pension, which during
the unsettled times of the Revolution had not been
paid. She wrote a letter to the Citizen Minister of Fine
Arts, in April, and says that she has been three
months in Paris vainly endeavouring to get the two
pensions which she had earned and obtained more
than twelve years before the Revolution. He must
know all about her claim, she says, because of the
number of complaints she has already made. Her
pensions are the result of "her study, work, and
talent," and therefore she argues she has virtually
paid for her pension quite as much as though she
had purchased government securities. The form of
government may change, and the change has been
for the better, as all the French will testify, but they
will not continue to do so if faith is not kept with
the public. As the Republic guaranteed the safety
of the person and property of every citizen, and was
founded on the rights of man, she considers herself
as a member of a great family, and is not afraid

to say she is quite worthy in every way of the title, and therefore she demands in the name of " law, equity, and justice", that her pension, which forms a portion of her revenue, shall be deemed as inalienable as a government annuity.

This appeal produced no better effect than its predecessors, and on 3rd June she wrote to a friend whom she had asked to act for her, reproaching him that he had forgotten " the poor recluse of Paraclet-Sophie—that Arnould who was formerly—at least in the words of one of our poets—the only goddess of the theatre of the gods."

Alexandrine had died before this date it would appear, and to add to Sophie's other troubles she had to keep the two children Alexandrine had borne to Murville. He was unable to look after them, as he was a soldier in the Army of the Pyrenees. But somebody procured for the eldest child—a boy—admission to the National School at Liancourt. Sophie writes to thank this friend " with all her heart, soul and strength for having made three persons happy—the father, the son and herself." Her gratitude is " without prejudice to that of Murville, who is capable of speaking for himself."

Shortly after Sophie was back at Luzarches. She did not yet despair of getting her pension, and was again writing to the Minister (26 July, 1797) She is still an unpaid creditor of the nation—a position which causes her "to live with indignation and die

of hunger," so that she has hardly the strength to
sign herself "most fraternally your affectionate con-
citoyenne, Sophie Arnould."

A severe illness came on shortly after the date of this
letter, as is shown by the following letter to Belanger.

"From Paraclet Sophie, 14 Brumaire, year 5 (November 4th, 1797).

"How can it be possible, my bel ange, you the
best and oldest of my friends, that I have been so
seriously and dangerously ill for more than four
months, without having heard the slightest word,
or receiving the slightest mark of interest or friendship from you? I should not have believed it, if
I had not experienced it. Ah! your heart must
reproach you.... These then are the friends of
the world. Besides during thirty-five days I had for
company the hideous creature called Death. Ah
well! I have no regret at the thought of depart-
ing ... I have been through a trial which has
proved to me that it is more difficult to live than
to die, but upon my word, that which I was
ignorant of were the ills caused by a fever—putrid,
bilious and malignant—now I know them in reality.
I have at last, thank God, a little strength, but am
still very weak, for I can scarcely walk; there are
some days when I have tried to drag along to
the garden door, to breathe the sun and air. Oh!
they were obliged to quickly bring me back to my

hovel, which measures nine feet square though which I can hardly walk across; perhaps I shall do so by and bye, but the present season is not too favourable to convalescents.

"I have one great consolation, and that is the active and tender interest that good Father Poupard has taken in my condition. I have found in him the heart of Dorval, and the generosity of Comte Lauraguais! Nevertheless the poor devil is in great pecuniary difficulties, none of his affairs are settled, there is still a sequestration upon his revenues, etc., etc. I have also to add to the name of this excellent friend, those of friends Darlet, François de Neufchateau, Mirbeck, Citoyenne La Chabaussière, and relations and others who have given me proofs of their interest, and surround me with the utmost care. My eldest son brought me a doctor from Paris, but I kept to my own village doctor, a true Sganarelle, singing always 'Bottle, my darling', and seldom leaving it No matter, he has nursed me well, treated me well, and cured me, and perhaps a doctor from Paris would not have cured me so well of a dangerous and complicated illness. I forgot to add another merit to my Esculapius, which is that he is mad at every new moon; but very mad during its continuance, or for four days at the least.

"Well, all this does not matter; if his art is in question, he gets back all his reason; he is the

greatest botanist that I know, and he has employed
nothing but medicinal plants to cure me, but I
believe he has the secrets of nature in this branch
of study.

"Adieu, my bel ange, I think enough has been
said by a poor girl who is so weak that she can
with difficulty use her limbs, and whose head is still
dizzy from illness, low diet, and all the rest of it.
I will not embrace you nor love you with all my
strength, for that would badly express how much
and how tenderly attached to you is your good
SOPHIE.

"P.S. Do not forget to remember me to
your charming and amiable companion, although I
feel the neglect she has shewn to her best and
oldest friend. She ought to have thought, nevertheless, that being so bewitched (*coiffée*) with her
as I am, it gives me great pain.

"With regard to coiffure, ah! I have even now
beautiful hair; if you saw me, you would say,
'See how beautiful she is, thin as a skeleton, pale
as death!' Ah, mon bon Dieu. What are we....,
to grow old, without being able to expect any more
spring times, pleasures, or love. With regard to
all that, tell all my good friends of the happy past,
Bourgainville, Sainte-Foy, Moyreau etc., etc., that
Sophie is still happy in her remembrance of them,
and that she embraces them with an old face but
with a heart always young, and which will never

grow old in friendship or tenderness; a sentiment which makes me strongly believe in the immortality of the soul, and that when we die we only change our shell, like the silk-worms."

One of the persons mentioned in this letter—François de Neufchateau—proved a good friend to Sophie, and it was by his means that the actress was enabled to enjoy a little comfort during the last days of her life.

In the fragments of her Memoirs she gives a short sketch of his career, which is doubtless true on the whole, though possibly some of the details may have been exaggerated.

According to her account, François de Neufchateau was the son of a small squire living in the Vosges. Some of Voltaire's works fell in his way whilst he was still quite a boy, and aroused within him a longing to be a great poet. When he was only thirteen or fourteen, he ran away from home, and made his way to Ferney, in order to worship at the shrine of the glorious patriarch of literature. Voltaire hardly appreciated the compliment, for he wanted to live retired from the world, and did not care to be bothered by literary aspirants just entering their teens. However, he read some of the verses which the boy showed him, pronounced them charming, and as a short way of getting rid of his visitor, suggested that the youth should make his way to Paris, where his literary talents would soon procure him fame.

Young de Neufchateau had sense enough to see that he needed some passport into literary society, and asked the old poet to give him some letters of introduction.

Voltaire knew better than to give the lad an introduction to one of the leading literary men of the day, and therefore furnished him with two letters of recommendation; — one to a Duchess who had been dead some years, and the other to Sophie Arnould.

François came to Paris, and finding that his one letter of introduction was of no use, went to Sophie. The actress was then getting old, and her reputation was on the wane. She saw that the boy, though awkward and half-educated, was in earnest, and that he had a great admiration for pretty women in general, and pretty actresses in particular.

Sophie took an interest in him, laughed at his follies, encouraged his ambition, gave him good sound practical advice of a worldly order, and took some pains to rid him of the villainous provincial accent which grated on her ears. The natural consequence was that he fell in love with her, and offered her his heart. She told him that she had too much sense to believe in the calf-love of a boy, and he was offended and would see her no more. When the Revolution broke out, some years later, young de Neufchateau became one of the warmest partisans of Liberty and Equality, and a fulsomely flattering ode, addressed to Robespierre, procured him such advancement that he became Minister of the Interior.

Sophie Arnould was then in poverty and distress, and remembering how she had befriended the Minister when he was a callow youth, she hoped he would assist her.

She went to the Luxembourg, and after waiting a long time amidst a crowd of place-hunters, sent in her name. Being seated near the door, which had been left open, she heard all that went on in the Minister's private room, and she heard him say,

" What does the old fool want. Tell her I am not in."

This was more than Sophie could stand. She bounced into the room and cried,

" I have not come to speak of the past; all that I want is that you should prevent me from dying in the hospital. The present is in your hands, but no one has any control over the future. Grant me the pension which was accorded me—unless you have cancelled it. And finally, Monsieur le Directeur, let me tell you that if I am an old fool, it is not my age that has made me a fool.—It was when I was young that I did foolish things."

The shaft went home; the Minister came forward, apologised, and promised that he would do all in his power for the ex-actress.

Perhaps he would have kept his promises, but Sophie went and related the incident to all her acquaintances, and the Opposition papers soon published

scathing articles about the pride and ingratitude of
the Minister.

A couple of years later he seems to have felt
some compunction for his behaviour, and having
heard, possibly from Belanger, to what straits she
was reduced, assisted her Most probably it was he
who sent Murville's son to school; at all events he
was asked to do so, and from the following pretty
little letter it would seem that the child's removal
to school was due to him, or Sophie would not
have troubled him with all the questions concerning
the outfit, etc.

"From Paraclet Sophie, 25 Prairial, year 5 (June
13th, 1797).

"Here I am once more at home, good and worthy
citizen, waiting the performance of your promises
of the place which I have solicited for the child of
one of your confrères (Murville), a man of letters,
and defender of his country, for the school at
Liancourt. I do not wish to trouble you too much,
citizen, but I regret the time which this youth has
already lost; he is twelve years old, and does not
know his A. B. C.

"His mother might perhaps be reproached for
this unpardonable negligence; she who had much
wit, knowledge, talents, etc., but she is no more!
and on account of the absence of his father, and
my particular sentiments for the memory of his

mother—whom I so much loved, that I cannot think of her without my eyes filling with tears—I become importunate to you

"Dare I, citizen, hope from your kindness and your well known complaisance, that you will let me hear about what I have asked you, and that you will also add two words of instruction as to what I shall have to do for the child, both for his little outfit, and how I shall send him to Liancourt. If I must have him taken there, or if the little band all go together.

"How I wish you would visit this little canton, and come to the poor little manor house of Sophie; you would be very welcome, and well received. You would not find a pretty face, but the kind face of a hostess; you would not have a sumptuous repast, but a good soup of cabbage and bacon, good vegetables, wine of our own growth, pure beautiful water, very clean, fine, white linen, and a good bed; that is all, but given with a good heart, since it will be that of

"SOPHIE ARNOULD."

We know absolutely nothing of Sophie's life at this period except what she tells us herself, which will be found related in the following letters which she addressed to Belanger.

"*To Belanger.* From Paraclet Sophie, the 4th Nivose, year 5 (December 23rd, 1797).

16

"I will only answer you in a few words to-day, my dear friends, and they must suffice you for the present, to express the gratitude which I feel for the tender sentiments which you expressed for me in the last letter which I received from you, for my health is not yet good, nor my strength sufficiently returned for me to be able to undertake to thank you as I feel I wish to do. I have been ill, yes, very ill, for fifty-three days...., but for thirty-five days I suffered agonies. Well, my bel ange, if your Sophie's fate had been decided, as you were always in her thoughts she would have preserved on the other side of death the memory of the tender and sincere attachment which she has always felt for you since her young days, but since I still live, nothing has altered in the sentiments of your always very loving

" Sophie.

"A thousand thanks on my part to your amiable secretary, in seeing her, in reading her letters I feel that it would be impossible to my heart, if she had not already become my rival for her to become so; but since fate has decided otherwise, we are better as we are, for in the future the three will be as one, here is already mine, which has taken its place in both of yours. Adieu, I charge it to embrace you, with all its power

"I should like to see you, my bel ange, but I am

in a difficulty about my arrangements, I wish to occupy a room in my large building, and, in order to procure the means, I have let as a farm the side of the building in which I live; I will tell you all that when my head is clearer, and I have less difficulty in writing, for I still hold my pen as Arlequin, the paralytic barber, held his razor.

"Put off the visit that you wish to make me until the spring, and then there will be splendid days for me.

"Remember me a thousand times to my friends, Sainte-Foy, and Bougainville.

"I must tell you that I am very pleased with the conduct of the Count of Lauraguais towards me; he came to my aid in a manner worthy of him."

"Sophie Arnould to Belanger, her best friend From Paraclet, the 19th Thermidor, 6th year (August 6th, 1798).

"Well! my bel ange, you say nothing to me of your visit to our illustrious friend, François de Neuf-château! You believe then that I have become in-different to all which concerns you? You are wrong, you are doubly wrong, you are trebly wrong, you are like the good man Pincé. If I had not been ill and had to keep my bed for a fortnight, on account of a cursed fever which proceeded from a dreadful cold, I should have gone to Paris myself to execute your commission, for I have always ready feet and a willing heart for my friends. Adieu, I cannot write to you longer, the cough which persecutes me, does not allow me to do any more. I cough with all my strength, but I love you with all my heart, and it is still stronger.

"Embrace your amiable companion for me, and, if I possess any physical strength, I will return it, interest and principal.

"SOPHIE."

"*To Belanger.* 8 Nivôse, year 8 (January 29th, 1800).

"Ah, my bel ange, you are always the same for goodness, generosity, and such a good heart! I would thank you sincerely, my poor friend, but what expressions can I employ!....They would always fall short of my gratitude, not for the money but for the kindness of the action.

"Ah! What good you have done my heart; here are a hundred years of happiness for me, if I had them to live. Console yourself, my friend, I have still a few pence, and have no want of the two louis that you have sent me, and of which you have deprived yourself for me, for I also know what your position is, but I will keep this piece to wear upon my heart, and will wear it until my death. I know the motto I shall put there, it shall be my relic. Good-bye, my bel ange, my good angel, my true friend, believe me there does not exist on earth a being who is more tenderly attached to you, and more inviolably attached to you than your

" SOPHIE ARNOULD"

" On the 24th I shall be with my good friends, with you, and your wife, and devote that day to my happiness."

Some one had doubtless suggested that Sophie was entitled to ask for a benefit at the Opera, and she therefore writes to Lucien Bonaparte soliciting that favour. But Lucien Bonaparte was far too much taken up with his own pleasures to pay much attention to the duties of his office, and in fact lost his place a few months later and was sent as Ambassador to Spain.

" Paris, 1st Pluviose, 8th year of the Republic. To the Minister of the Interior, Lucien Bonaparte (Jan. 21, 1800).

" CITIZEN MINISTER,

" My name is Sophie Arnould, perhaps quite unknown to you, but formerly very well known at the Théâtre des Dieux.

" I will not, however, Citizen Minister, take up your time and weary you with a long preamble in order to tell you of my twenty-six misfortunes. I had already taken the liberty to address my complaint to our First Consul, but I have just been informed in a newspaper that he can only be approached

through you, my Minister; so I said to myself: Be
satisfied, Sophie! He has a kindred heart, tell him
your history, and it will be the same as if I said
it to your elder. Since my youngest years, and without any other destiny than the chance which governs
all things, twenty years of my life have been con-
secrated to the Théâtre des Arts, where some natural
talents, and a careful education and instruction, procured me the support of people of taste, scholars,
artists, in short, persons justly celebrated. As for
me, I had then to recommend me, a prepos-
sessing appearance, extreme youth, vivacity, soul, a
mischievous disposition, and a good heart: these are
the auspices under which I was fortunate enough to
make my life illustrious, and obtain a sort of celebrity,
glory, fortune, and many friends. Alas! to-day my
luck has turned; as to the celebrity, my name is
still cited with praise in *Psyché*, *Thélaire*, *Iphigénie*,
Eglé, *Pomone*, in a word, at the Théâtre des Arts....
As to the friends, I can only tell you that I so well
deserved them, that I have only lost those whom
death has removed from me, and the axe of the
decemvirate has deprived me of; there is thus only
inconstant fortune, which, without rhyme or reason,
has given me the slip. In these circumstances then
I am too old for Love, and too young for Death.

"You see then, Citizen Minister, how cruel it is,
after so much happiness, to be reduced to so miserable
a state, and, after having kindled so much fire, to be

to-day without even a faggot to burn in my chimney; for the fact is, that since the nation has put my name on its ledger, I have nowhere to sleep, and nothing to live on. I assuredly do not ask for riches, but only enough to enable me to live and to avoid an unhappy old age; I have some heavy expenses, because in my fortunate days I supported the poor members of my family. That had to be; but my poverty does not make them rich. Therefore, Citizen Minister, I ask you to come to my aid, and to continue those benefits which my friend François de Neufchâteau, when he became Minister, procured for me; I owe this testimony to his heart.

" In the list of annuities which he gave to the artists, I was put down for a sum of two hundred francs a month.... Vouchsafe to continue it. I should still have a favour to ask you, and which favour has for example those of my old comrades, to whom it has been granted; that is a performance for my benefit at the Théâtre des Arts, but is it true, as they say, that I must charge myself with a principal part, and disguise myself as *Thélaire*, *Iphigénie*, etc., etc.? Oh! that is impossible: it would render me as ridiculous as Mme Covet:

" *As Venus! my dear, as Venus!* "

" Therefore, Citizen Minister, I await from you all that I have a right to obtain; all that misfortune expects from a good and tender soul like yours.

You are too young to know me, but many of your friends — scholars, men of letters, and artists who surround you—formerly composed my society; they will tell you who Sophie is, but such praise as they give me will not tell you enough if they do not express the sentiments of admiration, of love, and profound respect, with which I am penetrated, for my country, our laws, and your virtues.

"SOPHIE ARNOULD."

Here is another letter to the same person, a little later.

"Sophie Arnould. To the Citizen Minister of the Interior.

"CITIZEN MINISTER,

"I salute you, and thank you for what you have done for my comrades and for me—all of us poor veterans of the Théâtre des Arts—in securing to us permanently the payment of two hundred francs a month, which had been previously granted to us provisionally; it now only remains to us to beg you to complete this favour by signing the document which will secure it to us, and which the Treasury wants in order to discharge it. As to the second demand, which is personally mine (for the performance for my benefit at the Théâtre des Arts), and which you have refused, Citizen Minister, I will wait, as you wish, until a happier time for the performance, and surely then the absurd obstacle which prevails, of appearing in person at such a representation, will no longer exist.

"Salutation and profound respect

"SOPHIE ARNOULD."

"Tuesday, 19th Ventôse, year 8 of the S R. F. (March 10th, 1800)."

In order to obtain this benefit performance, Sophie writes as follows to Cellerier, the manager of the Opera.

"From Paraclet Sophie, Commune de Luzarches, department de Seine et Oise. The 17th Messidor, year 8 (July 6th, 1800).

"You promised me, my amiable and very old friend, your good offices, relative to my interests, and I claim them, for I find myself in such an embarrassed condition that I am obliged to live like a poor unhappy wretch, and am obliged to stay at home, and deprive myself of everything. You know, my friend, that there remains owing to me from the provisional help which I at present receive from the coffers of the Opera, the last two months, Ventôse and Germinal. You ought to make them pay me the two together, which would be of more use to me than getting it in small sums, which is the usual way. Oh, good Heavens! my dear friend, how vexed I am to worry you about that

avarice, for that is what it is; if I had not enjoyed
so much prosperity formerly, so much esteem, and
all that constitutes the charm of life, I should not
to-day find myself so poor and unhappy; but,
alas! to find myself growing old in want and in
misery, and to be condemned to put up with every
privation, is a sad way to finish life. If I could sing
still, I could easily sing like Lise, in some comedy
from the Italian—I do not remember which,—

> Ca ne devait pas finir par là
> Puisque ça commençait comme ça

"Ah! my friend, perhaps you remember still the
old times. At any rate they were good times; there
were slaves, it is true, but they were our own.
We have pigs now instead, and really, my friend,
between ourselves, I do not like the species. I do
not find them amusing; they are not worth anything;
it all displeases me more than I can express.

"I very well know that, if we have not that which
we like, we must like that which we have; but I
have nothing. At least let us have money!

"This is what I wish for you, my friend, it is also
what I ask from you; so be it; upon this, I salute
you, and embrace you as heartily as I love you.

"SOPHIE ARNOULD."

"P.S. It is said in our hamlet that Bonaparte
has returned to Paris, and therefore that glory and
happiness follow him! write to me, my friend, answer

my letter; even if it be a refusal, at least your letter will charm my dulness, for an old shepherdess has not very much to amuse her."

In April, 1801, Lucien Bonaparte has given place to Chaptal, and Sophie writes to him as follows.

"Sophie Arnould to Citizen Chaptal, Minister of the Interior.

"CITIZEN MINISTER,

"I see very well that with you 'to promise' is 'to give.' I have already felt the good effects of your kindness to me; it is very pleasant for me to render you my gratitude. My mind will be much more embarrassed than my heart, if you will not be the interpreter of my feelings; on this occasion you have promised to our friends that you will continue your favours, and that you will not lose sight of poor Sophie; I count upon you. You have taught me too well not to doubt your promises; I will only tell you, citizen minister, that my wants are extremely pressing. I wait the moment when I can see you, to testify by word of mouth my grateful sentiments, as well as the profound esteem which I have for you.

"SOPHIE ARNOULD."

" *To Belanger.*

"From Paraclet Sophie, the 6 Nivôse, year 9 (27 December, 1800).

"I have received a letter from you, my bel ange, as kind, sweet, and amiable as yourself, and it has made my heart joyful, by the evidences of attachment which you have given in it, which not only has given me courage to support a solitary life full of privations, to which I am condemned by the loss of my fortune, the unhappy result of misfortune of the time and the circumstances, and the events so horrible and numerous towards the end of our century, but you have made my heart once more feel hope and consolation. I have once more experienced happiness. I replied to your letter at once, thanking you greatly for the two pounds that you informed me of, and which I also received....That is all well and good, but a long time has already passed since that, and I am very wretched at not having received any news of you since then; and the event which has just happened at Paris renders me still more anxious to hear from you, therefore, my dear friends, let me at once have news of you. I send my maid expressly to your house, to bring me back the most certain tidings of you. I do not ask for any other news than about yourselves, and if anything has happened to you, and if chance has not drawn you, as well as your affairs, to the quarter where this abominable catastrophe happened; and if there is any friend of yours or mine among the victims. Oh, good heavens! What abominable people! What an expedient to get rid of a single man, and moreover what a man!...a man to

whom we owe the peace and happiness which we
enjoy. Well, my friends, I am enraged at my power-
lessness against such wretches; my son in the army,
my hussar, has well avenged us with the army of the
Rhine against the Austrians. He and his companions
in arms, let it be understood, have made them bite
the dust; in the last affair which took place at He-
benstenden, and Malskerden, beyond the defile of St.
Christophe, they took from those cruel enemies a
park of artillery of 87 pieces of cannon, and 200
wagons full of ammunition; the loss of their men is
estimated at from 16, to 17.000, and as many
wounded, or prisoners, and without exaggeration!
for, according to Brancas, the commander of the
garrison at Munich, where the prisoners have been
taken, has himself already counted 9.800, and every
day more prisoners are being brought in from all
parts. The woods are full of people, and wild
frightened horses who do not know which way to
turn, the roads are strewn with the dead and wounded;
and there are not enough carriages to transport these
latter. On our side, Brancas estimates the loss at
3.000 men, he has also added, 'It was not a battle,
it was simply a butchery.' Charlot, our Prince de
Ligne, is amongst the number of prisoners for the
third time, according to his usual fashion; it is a
little friendly service apparently, which he must have
rendered to our friend....but hush! no more joking!
other times, other cares! Be quiet, Sophie!—after

all, to return to the subject, the enemy have lost
two generals, and two others are prisoners. Listen
to our brave hussar, who can say like La Rissole
du *Mercure galant* 'I have even contributed a little
to their death.'

'Take notice that all this loss of enemies falls on
the best troops and soldiers, upon the pick of the
army; all batallions of grenadiers! they came, attacked
us, and we were also on the right (the 9th hussars),
and we attacked, defended, with great success, and
without loss. I embrace you tenderly; dry your
tears, my good and tender mother. I beg of you
to tell this great and joyful news to all your friends.
As you always place citizen Belanger first among
them as well as his amiable and clever wife, will you
charge yourself at the same time with remembering
me to them,—my affectionate friendship to the
husband, my respects and homage to the wife, and
if you like, a slight reminder from the hussar to
the agreeable women of their society.'—I have no
more paper, and have only room for the place I
would occupy in your heart, to tell you that you
can count to her last sigh upon the heart of your
very loving   Sophie."

"P S Madame Belanger ought to write and let
me hear about you both a little oftener. She who
has so good a heart, should not forget the unhappy."

One slight happiness brightened the last days of

poor Sophie's life. François de Neufchateau remembered the service she had done him when he first arrived in Paris and offered her a room in his hotel and a pension of 200 francs a month.

She abandoned Luzarches and came to Paris, and spent the few remaining months of her life in the city, where she was able to get good medical advice and enjoy some degree of comfort in her last illness. It is from this address that she writes to Belanger.

"Paris, 13 Floréal, year 9, (May 3rd, 1801).

"How good you are, my friends, how kind you are, my bel ange, what a good heart! how pleased I am that I have always given you preference in my heart, to everything else that exists in the world. If you knew how affected I am at your kind offers. Oh! you who know so well how to read my heart, you who know so well how to understand me, I leave to your heart the task of guessing mine: it is always the same for you.—Of the whole of me, nothing is changed but the sheath. My health is always very miserable. The learned Esculapians, Pelletan of the Hotel-Dieu, and Boyer of la Charité, have paid me a visit, and think that I have need of courage and firmness. Dr Michel has to carry out this cure, and we shall see. I am like Valein of the 'False Infidelities', I wait. It is hard for a woman of spirit, when peace is announced in our low countries, to see the enemy come and establish itself in her own. Ah! Sophie deserved a better fate....once more the poor stupid....not a bit of it, nor even if I grieve over it, how will that improve me? No faith! I will accept my lot bravely: at the end of the ditch, the fall. However, it may be I am going to take care of myself and get cured, if it be the good pleasure of these gentlemen.

"I accept your proposal, my dear friends, and when the necessity arises I will ask you, since you will have it so. Keep well, and always love me, that is the most sovereign specific for my ills that I know of. What greater happiness than to be loved by those we love. As for me, I love you, and seal this avowal with a very tender kiss.

"P.S. I have not yet seen the good and handsome Vigier; he has promised to come and see me, and I reckon upon him. As I keep my room, I look forward to seeing you, my dear friends, either morning or evening, whenever you have time, for I know well that you have much to occupy you, and at the time when we ought to be thinking of nothing but rest, we must work to live. Ah! that is very nice! I have to work to mend my washing tub,¹ since the gods so order it.... it will not be of much use to me, but after all, we never know

---

¹ An allusion to a story which is to be found in *The Golden Ass*, Boccaccio, Molini, and other writers, and which La Fontaine had rendered popular in France.

what may happen. The end of this century has
been so prolific in miracles, that the beginning of
another may also have its prodigies. There! good-
bye, good-bye, my poor ! ⁴ ⁺ I will love you till
death, and I hope to still live a long time

⁎.   ⊦   ⅃   ⅃.   ⁎.   ⁊   ƭ   ⁎

"Well it is not certain that I shall be cured, and
we shall see ..."

" *To Belanger.*

"Paris, 11th Prairial, year 9 (May 31, 1801).

" Good-day, my dear friends, I am always in
terrible pain, but the remedies have worked miracles.
After all, there is nothing to do but have courage.
So my physicians tell me. That which gives it to
me more than anything in the world, is to know
myself beloved by you, and that the life I am
trying to preserve is of interest to you Always
love me, and do not pity me too much, for I am
happy at the present moment, I have just received
a letter from my hussar, from my Constant, from
that son who is so cherished by me, and who so
well deserves all my tenderness. And, as if he had
guessed all your goodness to me, and what friends
I have had in the husband and wife, he has told
me some things specially for you, he has asked
me to recall him to your memory in such friendly
and tender terms, that I really cannot express them.
Rest assured, my friends, that no one has had more

17

tender feelings for you, than have the son and the
mother   "SOPHIE ARNOULD."

" P.S.   If pain did not make me so often leave
off writing, I should have much more to say to
you, but these ladies are imperious, and must be
obeyed.   However, I cannot pass over in silence the
homage and evidences of respect and attachment
which he has avowed for Madame Breteuil."

" *To Belanger.*

" Paris, 14th Thermidor, year 9 (August 2nd, 1801).

" Good-day, my good and bel ange, how are
both of you, your wife and yourself?   I do not ask
you if you are happy, for who is so, or who can
be so, at the present time, except the knaves, the
blackguards, and the careless !   I confine myself to
asking news of your health, in which I take more
interest than in my life.   In respect to health, you
will scold me well, I think, if I do not tell you all
about my own.   Well! it continues to improve.
The tumour is sensibly diminishing, although it is
far from being quite at an end, it was besides so
considerable that I regard as a miracle the beneficial
operation which has been the cause of the remedy.
I am now taking 72 grains of hemlock; lotions,
fumigations, injections, three or four times a day,
according as the pain requires, but it is a hard
business, and I should like to be well rid of it;
and to add to it, there are the medicines which

have to be taken as a broom to cleanse the body, etc., etc. Oh, good Heavens, what we come to. My friend, I assure you that I should give up these painful remedies if I were not attached to life by sentiments of maternal tenderness for my Constant, and by the most loving friendship for two or three friends, of whom you will always be the first in my heart.

"I do not know, my friend, if your people have told you that I sent back, about a week ago, fifteen bottles (empty be it understood) which you had sent me full, which is to say that I have no more: nevertheless I can very well do without, in fact, I want it so little, that I will not bother you, nor be troublesome about it, especially as directly I receive some money from the Minister of the Interior (where they do not pay me always, they treat me as if I were asking for alms) I shall purchase a cask of Macon, which I rather like, and it will serve to supply me for a year, since I have been so badly treated in money matters that I have not enough money left to keep even a cat.

"I am expecting my son Constant; a letter which I have received from Citizen Noel, prefect at Colmar, where the regiment of Brancas is in cantonment, has just given me the information. I do not know if the rumours which are circulating of the descent upon England, and the preparations which are being made with such vigour, will not change this project,

for our hussar is always anxious to fight for his
country, and to go where he hopes for glory; in
that case, and if he come to Paris, you may be
sure that his first care will be to renew, my dear
Belanger, the sentiments of friendship which have
reigned in his heart for you since his tenderest
infancy.

"I cannot tell you any more of the sister of Constant, my dear friend, since she is no more, but I
will tell you of the daughter of this dear deceased.

"I have seen M. Vigier, who has assured me that he
will very soon rid me of that troublesome person....
he has received the warrant which he was waiting
for, and he will hasten her departure. It is what
I heartily wish for, and have long wished for; I
count the moments which will bring me this good
fortune.

"M. Vigier has given me to understand that he
has no money to give me just now, to which I
have replied eagerly: 'Oh! that does not matter,
provided that you have enough to send her away
at once.' You will oblige me greatly, my dear
friend, to urge upon this good, kind man to hasten
this departure. As this little girl is at Luzarches,
it will be necessary to know exactly the time of
the departure, so that she may be found at the
place named for the carriage which will take her
to her father; this is what I beg of you to see.
after. I also entreat of you to send as soon as

possible to take the Persian furniture which I have
at home, and destined by me for that dear Santeny,
and that by agreement also made with your dear
wife; I hurry you about that, because I have sent
for some furniture from my cottage, and a bed,
which I shall place in my drawing-room here, for
my poor hussar, should he come to Paris, so that
I may have him as near me as possible If you
have some old chairs to spare, you may send them
to me, or arm-chairs; the whole for convenience,
having renounced for a long time, Satan, his pomps,
and his works. There¹ here is a long letter, but
it is always like that, when we write to those we
love we can never finish, there are always a hundred
thousand things to say Farewell, I embrace you,
I embrace your wife, and I love you.

"SOPHIE ARNOULD."

"Kind wishes to your pretty neighbour."

Occasionally Sophie varies her correspondence by
writing a letter to Mme Belanger.

"To Madame Bélanger.   Paris, 8th Fructidor, year
9 (26 August, 1801).

" But what has become of you, my good friends,
that I hear nothing about you? If I had legs, or
at least any way of coming, I would at once run
to you.   So come yourself to see me, my kind friend.

I have no end of things to tell you. Firstly,
do not expect to find me at the same place where
you left me, that is to say in the large apartment on the first floor of the Maison Angivilliers.
I am on the floor beneath, at least I mean on the
entresol of Number 11, but on the same staircase.
The premises are smaller, less expensive to live in,
and therefore more suited to my present distress.
That is one of my reasons, the other, or rather the
others, proceed from the desire to please an amiable
woman, one who is made to adorn her name by her
talents. I allude to Madame Benoist. She is young,
amiable and witty; she is the mother of a family,
and a woman of talent. I will tell you the rest by
word of mouth. The rooms which I occupy at present being much smaller than the former ones, I
must ask you if you will kindly disembarrass me
of this Persian furniture, which we have already
arranged was to be taken to your country house.
I shall not have to consider how to replace it,
because a half dozen straw chairs will answer my
purpose at present. But the most inconvenient thing
of all to me is this Clementine, whom my friend
Vigier does not hurry himself to rid me of. I beg
of you, my good friends, to try and make him keep
his promise as soon as possible. If M. Vigier has
no money to give me he will not give it, but I hope
that he will at least have the goodness to spare me
the daily expense I am put to for this little girl;

in the straitened position I am in, I feel unable to increase my expenses. One must have a pension to pay every month the expenses for the keep, which are bound to be considerable, on account of her want of care, cleanliness, order, etc. So therefore, my good friends, have a little pity for your poor

"SOPHIE ARNOULD."

"Just a word in reply, if only to tell me where you are, what you are doing and if you are both in good health.

"P.S. A thousand kind regards to your charming neighbour Madame de Breteuil.

"I am expecting her constant adorer, our brave hussar, he is going to make a high holiday, in order to go and kiss your hands, as soon as he arrives in the fine City of Paris. Town is not the word, any longer, it is the Commune. Well! *that* for the Commune. But he will come to see you, who are friends who are not common."

It will be remarked that throughout the years in which Sophie was in such great poverty and distress, we hear nothing of the Comte de Lauraguais. She had been more than a mistress to him, and had borne him four children. She loved him deeply and sincerely at one time, and would no doubt have continued to do so if his violence, fickleness, and eccentricities had not estranged her affection.

Yet she never wholly forgot him. She remembered the days when, as the painter Dorval, he had won her heart, and the memory of the time when each kiss had to be paid for with a hundred tears still clung to her.

That he did not assist her to any extent in her misery is strange, but is perhaps capable of explanation. He was never a *persona grata* with the Court, either in the days of Louis XV or Louis XVI, and was always in disgrace and often in exile. Had he been only a private citizen we should no doubt have found him in the front rank of the leaders of the Revolution at some period, though his lack of fixity of purpose would have prevented him from retaining the position for any length of time. His antipathy to the Court doubtless served to preserve his head during the dangerous times of the Revolution, but he was an aristocrat, though a very liberal-minded one, and he lost all his property.

After the Revolution he retired to Manicamp, in the department of Aisne, where he bought or rented a small farm. As early as 1783 he had declared that he cared for nothing but " trees and fields, and his dear old Sophie," and in 1798 he invited her to share his retreat.

Sophie was unable to avail herself of the offer. She had, with great difficulty, obtained from the Government a small pension, and whilst she was on the spot she could manage by dint of personal ap-

plications, and the intercession of her friends to keep
the Minister up to his engagements, but she was
aware that if she left Paris she would be out of
mind as well as out of sight, and her pension would
inevitably be stopped.

She had come to Paris in 1797, and, being very
poor, had taken lodgings over a barber's shop in
the Rue du Petit Lion. François de Neufchateau
found her there, and remembering his unfulfilled
promises of three years before, had offered her a
lodging in his own house. Perhaps her presence
was inconvenient to him, or she felt that her position too much resembled that of a pensioner, and
might afford the Minister an excuse for stopping her
allowance, at all events she moved a few months
later to the Hotel d'Angivilliers, where she first
lodged in a large apartment, and afterwards moved to
a smaller and more comfortable suite of rooms in
the same house. She still retained possession of
the house at Luzarches and paid occasional visits
there, even as late as the end of the year 1800

It was while she was in this hotel, and seemingly
just at the time she was about to change her rooms,
that she wrote to "Citizen Brancas Lauraguais,
proprietor and farmer," to invite him to come
and live with her, since she was unable to go
to him.

The first half of the letter is mainly political, and
as he has doubtless not renounced politics, the best

and safest place for him would be Paris. He will
doubtless reply, she says, that money is required,
but as he has a little, and she has a little, they
can manage, as they will have no great expenses,
no rent to pay, they can breakfast at home, and
dine with their friends, and they will be discreet
when they are away from home, and quiet and sober
when they are at home.

She has also plenty of wood at Paraclet, and by
mutually helping each other, they can live like Baucis
and Philemon, and both could write books. If she
had more room, she would be more pressing in
her offer, but perhaps in a week she will have a
more comfortable apartment, but she can offer him
a good room of a fair size, airy, and well situated,
where he will be free to do as he likes, a private
door and staircase, a good bed, nice chairs and
chests of drawers, a large writing-table to hold all
his papers, etc., in fact all that he can need. She
has a servant—an unmarried woman, thirty years
of age, not very intelligent, but all the better for
that very reason, and a good worker.

But he will not need a servant, Sophie declares.
She will do all that he requires, and say as she
does so, " How happy I am to take off the boots
of one I love."

Lauraguais did not accept the invitation, most
probably because he felt that he would be sure to
take part in the politics of the day, and would

get into difficulties again. * He did, however, come to see Sophie, and as the following anecdote will prove, it must have been several months before her death, and whilst she still had some degree of strength and energy.

Some few years after the death of Sophie Arnould, three dramatic authors announced the performance of a new play, entitled *Les Amans sans jambes, ou les Amis de Mlle Arnould.* The piece was founded on an anecdote of her early life. She was sent to prison at Fort l'Evêque for a day, for having replied insolently to the Lieutenant of Police. She met in the prison a poor man who was imprisoned for debt. On her release she got up a raffle for a valuable gold chain—so many members at five louis each. With the money thus obtained she took the poor old man out of prison. The only person who suffered was the winner in the lottery, for the chain did not exist.

It was on this incident that the play was to be founded, but Lauraguais expected that he would be introduced into the piece, and a correspondence

* He survived Sophie many years and lived to be more than eighty years old. He was created a peer when Louis XVIII came to the throne, but he had a supreme contempt for many of his fellow peers, who were newly-created, and could not boast of such high descent On one occasion the Clerk of the House was calling over the names of the members, and came to that of the Duc de Brancas There was no response "Pas encore arrive," said the clerk and was about to pass on At that moment the old Duc entered the Chamber. "Pardon, monsieur," he called out, "il est arrive, mais il n'est pas *parvenu.*'

ensued on the subject between him and the authors. In one of these letters, he says that when Sophie was ill, a friend suggested that she needed some occupation or amusement to distract her mind, and Lauraguais therefore proposed to her that they should write their recollections together. Sophie replied that she had lost all her notes* and that even if she had preserved them she would burn them. Her reason for this was that the "ingrates" who would be mentioned would not deserve the celebrity they would attain, and those who were not mentioned did not deserve that she should do anything to amuse them.

"Such, Messieurs," concludes de Lauraguais, "were the words of Mlle Arnould. I do not very well see how you could put them into a vaudeville."

The end was fast approaching. Want, starvation, and mental anxiety had so weakened the constitution of Sophie Arnould that it is doubtful if she would have lived long even if she had been surrounded by every care. In addition to her other complaints she met with a fall which induced a scirrhous tumour of the rectum. She must have suffered terribly, and she had to undergo several painful, and useless, operations.

Though she was not quite in such distress as

This is not correct, unless we suppose her Memoirs to be not genuine.

she had been, she was still badly in want of money.
Lucien Bonaparte had promised her a free benefit
at the Opera; he afterwards withdrew the permission
but promised to give her 6 000 francs. Part of this
sum she did receive, but the balance did not come,
and she was obliged to ask Belanger to write to the
Minister, which he did in the following terms, on
11 Messidor of the Year X (30 June, 1802).

"CITIZEN MINISTER,

"I write this letter for you alone. It is written
from the bedside of the celebrated Arnould, who is
dying. * This woman dies deprived of relief that
her state of distress does not permit her to procure.
You granted her a performance for her benefit at
the Théâtre des Arts, and some kind persons offered
her 1.200 francs. You then desired that this permission should be withdrawn, and exchanged for an offer
to give her a sum of 6 000 francs. She has received
only 4.000. The 2 000 still due would be of the
greatest use to her, but to whom is she to address
herself to obtain the fulfilment of this promise. The
treasurer of the Théâtre des Arts declares that he
cannot pay the money without a special order
from you.

"And this unfortunate woman—of whom Gluck
said, 'If it had not been for the voice and elocution
of Mlle Arnould my *Iphigenia* would never have

* She lived nearly four months after this date.

been performed in France'—is now deprived of the means of prolonging her life, for want of pecuniary assistance.

"What would Moncrif, Rousseau, d'Alembert, Diderot, Helvetius, Baron d'Holbach, and all the other celebrated men who sought her society (as you will find in their correspondence) have said to this? What would Voltaire himself have said?—he who when at the age of ninety-two had himself carried to her house, and traced these lines on her bust;

> Ses grâces, ses talents ont illustré son nom,
> Elle a su tout charmer, jusqu'à la jalousie
> Alcibiade en elle eut cru voir Aspasie,
> Maurice, Lecouvreur, et Gourville, Ninon

"The woman who is thus neglected lived amongst our great men, she lived to help the unfortunate, she was a pattern to her pupils and all who aspire to success on the Stage in those parts which she adorned and even created; celebrated men have immortalised her talent and her wit, and yet she is dying for want of means to procure remedies for the cruel sufferings she endures."

We believe this letter was the means of shaming the Minister into paying the remainder of the sum due, and at least palliate her sufferings. But she gradually grew weaker, worn out with pain, and on the morning of 30 Vendemiaire in the year XI (22nd October, 1802) the curé of St Germain l'Auxerrois was sent for to give her the extreme unction.

When he had finished, and was about to leave the room he saw by a look in her expressive and still beautiful eyes, that she wished to speak to him.

He put his ear down to her mouth, and the words fell low and clear

"Quia multum amavit" [*]

—then all was still.

Her body was buried the next day, but we know not for certain where. M.M. de Goncourt think she must have been buried in Montmartre Cemetery, because all persons who died in the 1st Arrondissement were interred there, but either Belanger or Lauraguais might have caused her to be buried elsewhere. At all events no stone marks her last resting place.

Most of the newspapers made no mention of her death—those that did insert it confined themselves to a bare mention of the event contained in two or three lines The *Journal de Paris* knew or cared so little about her that it stated she died at Luzarches, the writer being unaware that she had resided in Paris during the latter part of her life.

The few effects she possessed at the time of her death were claimed by her sons and Murville, but the Tribunal de 1re Instance decided that, all her children being illegitimate, the money derived from

[*] St. Luke vii, v. 47

the sale of her furniture should be handed over to her brother.

Our task is ended, and here we take our leave of Sophie Arnould. We have traced her career from her birth to her unmarked, unknown grave, have recorded her stage triumphs, noted her most telling witticisms, chronicled her many failings and vices, and now leave her to the praise and blame of all who may care to peruse her history. There can be but little to praise and much to blame, but we may charitably hope that her last words proved true, and that her sins, which were many are forgiven, *quia multum amavit.*

THE END

Printed in Great Britain
by Amazon.co.uk, Ltd.,
Marston Gate.